Nehemiah

Also by James Montgomery Boice

NEHEMIAH

An Expositional Commentary

JAMES MONTGOMERY BOICE

BakerBooks
Grand Rapids, Michigan

Published in 2005 by Baker Books
a division of Baker Publishing Group
P.O. Box 6287, Grand Rapids, MI 49516-6287
www.bakerbooks.com

Paperback edition published in 2006
ISBN 978-0-8010-6640-5

Previously published under the title *Nehemiah: Learning to Lead* by Fleming H. Revell

Printed in the United States of America

The Library of Congress has cataloged the hardcover edition as follows:
Boice, James Montgomery, 1938–
     Nehemiah / James Montgomery Boice.
         p.   cm. — (Boice commentary series)
     Includes bibliographical references and index.
     ISBN 0-8010-1282-1 (cloth)
     1. Bible. O.T. Nehemiah—Commentaries. I. Title. II. Series: Boice, James
     Montgomery, 1938–   . Boice commentary series.
BS1365.53.B65 2005
222′.8077—dc22   2004014343

10   11   12   13   14   15   16   9   8   7   6   5   4   3

To Jesus Christ
the King of Kings and Lord of Lords
the Leader of Leaders

Contents

Preface

If I were an advertising executive writing promotional copy for the sale of the memoirs of Nehemiah, the governor of Judah during the second half of the fifth century BC, I would have an easy and pleasant task before me. Few Bible books address modern concerns so strongly and directly or are so practical. My copy would say things like this:

Be a leader
Learn how to:
    Gather information and form workable plans
    Get other people to do what you want them to do
    (and like doing it)
    Manage a difficult boss
    Motivate subordinates
    Master six great secrets for overcoming obstacles
    Succeed where others have failed
    Win without intimidation

Each of those items (and more) is taught in Nehemiah, but I am afraid if I limited myself to commending the book in that way, I would be missing the most important element. The most important thing about Nehemiah is that he was a man of God, and because he was close to God in prayer and personal piety, he was able to draw from God the wisdom, patience, skill, and perseverance he needed to complete his great task.

What a task it was! Nehemiah went to the ancient Jewish capital of Jerusalem from the Persian capital of Susa in 445 BC in order to rebuild the city. It had been destroyed 141 years before (in 586 BC) when Nebuchadnezzar, the king of Babylon, had attacked Judah and carried off most of its inhabitants. Jerusalem had been burned, and the great stones that made up the one-and-a-half- to two-and-a-half-mile-long wall of the city had been dislodged and tumbled into the steep valleys that surrounded it on all sides. Nothing of any value had been left. As the decades slipped by, grass and trees had grown up in the deserted streets and pathways, and refuse had covered the masses of the overthrown stones.

Moreover, the only people who were available to do the demanding work of reconstruction were exiles who had begun to return to Jerusalem nearly a century earlier. They had tried to build the wall then and on several later occasions, but they had failed each time and were thoroughly discouraged.

A difficult task?

More like impossible. But Nehemiah so planned the work and so motivated the frustrated and disheartened refugees that the task was completed, in spite of fierce and mounting opposition, in just fifty-two days. Nehemiah began to rebuild the wall on the first of August, 445 BC, and finished it on the twenty-first of September.

How did he do it? Nehemiah's testimony is that it was accomplished by God working through him and those others who assisted in the work. When he first asked the Persian king Artaxerxes for permission to go to Jerusalem to rebuild the city and Artaxerxes agreed—a small miracle in itself—Nehemiah did not boast of his skill in handling the emperor but said instead, "Because the gracious hand of my God was upon me, the king granted my requests" (Neh. 2:8). When he was opposed by Sanballat and Tobiah, two formidable enemies of his project, Nehemiah declared, "The God of heaven will give us success" (v. 20). When the wall was finished less than two months later, he testified strongly, "This work had been done with the help of our God" (Neh. 6:16).

Nehemiah had the skills of a great leader. We can learn from him again and again in this area. But even more important was his deep dependence on God, and we need to learn from that too.

It was my privilege to present these studies of Nehemiah to the Sunday evening congregations of Tenth Presbyterian Church in the fall of 1988, and I am thankful to many who were present for helpful comments and suggestions, some of which have been incorporated into the following chapters. As usual, I want to thank the congregation and session of Tenth Church for allowing me to spend so much time in studies of this nature, especially when there are many needs that could pull me in other worthwhile directions. I am thankful too for the excellent staff of the church who assist me by carrying on many of the church's other functions.

May God, who raised up Nehemiah, raise up many like him in our day. The church has seldom been in greater need of such leaders.

PART 1

Rebuilding the Wall

1

The First Dynamic: The Leader and God

Nehemiah 1:1–11

The words of Nehemiah son of Hacaliah:

In the month of Kislev in the twentieth year, while I was in the citadel of Susa, Hanani, one of my brothers, came from Judah with some other men, and I questioned them about the Jewish remnant that survived the exile, and also about Jerusalem.

They said to me, "Those who survived the exile and are back in the province are in great trouble and disgrace. The wall of Jerusalem is broken down, and its gates have been burned with fire."

When I heard these things, I sat down and wept. For some days I mourned and fasted and prayed before the God of heaven.

Nehemiah 1:1–4

Not far from where I live in Philadelphia, there is a modeling school that uses as its advertising slogan the words "Be a Model (or Look Like One)." In contrast to that slogan, I am not interested in having you or anybody else merely look like a leader, but I do want you to know what a real leader is and to become one.

Many people would like to be leaders, but most of them will never become leaders because of a great misunderstanding: *They think that leaders are born as leaders.* They do not know that leadership can and should be learned.

Vince Lombardi was a leader. He was the coach of the great Green Bay Packers football team, which he led to numerous national championships during his coaching tenure. He knew that leaders are made and said this about it:

> Leaders are made, they are not born; and they are made just like anything else has ever been made in this country—by hard effort. And that's the price that we all have to pay to achieve that goal, or any goal.
>
> And despite what we say about being born equal, none of us really are born equal, but rather unequal. And yet the talented are no more responsible for their birthright than the underprivileged. And the measure of each should be what each does in a specific situation.
>
> It is becoming increasingly difficult to be tolerant of a society which has sympathy only for the misfits, only for the maladjusted, only for the criminal, only for the loser. Have sympathy for them, help them, but I think it's also time for us to stand up for and to cheer for the doer, and the achiever, one who recognizes a problem and does something about it, one who looks for something extra to do for his country, the winner, the leader!

Today people are desperate for true leaders—in politics (on the national scene), in business, and in the church—since many we thought were leaders have let us down. Where are we to learn how to choose and be what we and so many others want? There are books on the subject. I think of Dale Carnegie's early and very successful classic, *How to Win Friends and Influence People.* There are Peter Drucker's helpful studies: *The Practice of Management, Managing for Results,* and *The Effective Executive.* Other less commendable books are *Winning through Intimidation* and *The One Minute Manager.*

I want to point you to the first book on leadership ever written. It is in the form of the memoirs of a man who served as governor of Jerusalem from 445 to 432 BC and whose name was Nehemiah.

Meet the Governor

Many people whose stories are told to us in the Bible were leaders. We usually think of the Bible as a book concerned only with the common man or with the lowly or disadvantaged, and it is. But that is only part of the story. For one thing, many of these "lowly" or "disadvantaged" people became leaders nevertheless. The New Testament apostles are examples. In addition, the recognized giants such as Abraham, Moses, Joshua, and David were leaders all the way. Much of the biblical story is about these outstanding people.

Nehemiah was one. He was a Jew, born in exile after the fall of Jerusalem to the Babylonians in 586 BC. He lived in a bad age so far as the destiny of his people was concerned. Yet like other Jews before him—Daniel and his three friends, Shadrach, Meshach, and Abednego, as well as Mordecai and his young ward Esther, who became the queen of Persia—Nehemiah rose to a position of influence in the court of the foreign king. Nehemiah was cupbearer to King Artaxerxes, as he tells us in Nehemiah 1:11 and 2:1.

The office of cupbearer sounds rather menial to us today, but this was not the situation. The office of cupbearer came about in ancient societies because of the danger that an emperor or king might be poisoned by some rival. The cupbearer was a trusted person appointed to care for and taste the wine to make sure it was safe before it was served to the king. Such a person was obviously highly esteemed and trusted to begin with. Because of his constant and regular access to the ruler, he naturally acquired influence far beyond all but a handful of other military leaders and nobles.

Moreover, in some periods of history the title "cupbearer" became more a title for one in a high position, like "chief of staff" or "cabinet minister," than a functional definition. The chief baker and chief cupbearer of Pharaoh held such high positions.

Another example is Thomas Chaucer, son of the famous early English poet Geoffrey Chaucer, author of *The Canterbury Tales*. He was a member of Parliament and four times speaker of the House of Commons. He is said to have fought at Agincourt under Henry V. This great soldier and parliamentarian became the chief butler of England under both Henry V and Henry VI, an honorary title for one who was close to the king.

In such a position many people might have been content to rest on their achievement or even retire to the good life, but Nehemiah showed his greatness as a leader at precisely this point. Although he was a man of the greatest possible influence in the Persian court, he left this enviable position to lead an effort to rebuild the walls of the city of Jerusalem, the city of his fathers, which now lay in ruins, and to restore its influence. He was successful against great odds.

Although others had been trying to rebuild Jerusalem's walls and thus restore the city's influence for nearly one hundred years, Nehemiah accomplished this Herculean task in only fifty-two days. Then he led a series of religious and moral reforms that were to have the greatest influence on the Jewish nation up to the time of Jesus Christ.

The book of Nehemiah is the record of this accomplishment.

History of the Times

The problem is presented to Nehemiah at the very beginning of the book (vv. 1–4). His brother Hanani (probably his actual brother, though the term could mean another Jewish man) and some other men came to the capital city of Susa, where Nehemiah was attending the king, and reported that the walls of Jerusalem were broken down and its gates burned with fire.

This had happened more than 140 years earlier, when Nebuchadnezzar had conquered Jerusalem and deported its population. But since that would be well known to Nehemiah and would hardly occasion a new outbreak of grief and fasting on his part, it is likely that the report referred to a second lesser destruction that seems to be alluded to in Ezra.

Understanding this requires knowing something of the history of this period. Here are some of the key events:

1. *The fall of Jerusalem to the Babylonians in 586 BC.* This event deserves special mention because it is the key to understanding most of what follows. We can see the importance of the fall of Jerusalem. The books of Ezra, Nehemiah, and Esther belong together in the Old Testament, and they are introduced with a quotation from the end of 2 Chronicles, which precedes them in the Bible. These verses concern the decree of King Cyrus of Persia to rebuild the temple in Jerusalem, which presupposes the city's fall. It is a way of showing that the fall of Jerusalem is the starting point for everything in these documents (cf. 2 Chron. 36:22–23; Ezra 1:1–3).

2. *The rise of Belshazzar as the last ruler of Babylon, replacing Nebuchadnezzar.* This change is reflected in Daniel 5, 7, and 8. Belshazzar was the son of Nebunaid, the last actual king of Babylon. But Nebunaid was absent from the city at the time of its fall to Cyrus, and it was therefore Belshazzar, who was in the city, who was actually overthrown.

3. *The fall of Babylon to Cyrus, the king of Persia, in 539 BC.* Cyrus was an unusually humane ruler. It was he who, in the first year of his reign, issued the decree permitting the Jews to return to their homeland to rebuild the temple. The first Jews returned in 538 BC under Zerubbabel and Joshua (the account is in Ezra 1–6). The foundations of the temple were laid at that time, but the work was opposed by the Samaritans and it was fifteen more years before the temple was completed.

4. *The reign of Darius the Mede.* Darius took the throne in 522 BC. He was the first Persian king to try to conquer Greece, but he was defeated at the Battle of Marathon (490 BC). The temple was actually completed during the reign of this man (between 520 and 515 BC), as attested to by the prophets Haggai and Zechariah.

Apparently, this was also when the Jews first tried to rebuild the wall and so provide for the city's defenses. The opening report in Nehemiah, "The wall of Jerusalem is broken down, and its gates have been burned with fire" (Neh. 1:3), probably relates to an effort by Rehum and Shimshai to defeat this first attempt, rather than to the original destruction of the wall by the Babylonians in 586 BC (cf. Ezra 4:23).

5. The reign of Xerxes, also known as Ahasuerus. Xerxes took the throne in 486 BC. He was the second Persian king to invade Greece (in 480 BC), but he was defeated at Salamis and Plataea. This is the man who chose Esther as his queen (in 479 BC).

6. The reign of Artaxerxes I Longimanus from 465 to 424 BC.

7. The arrival of Ezra in Jerusalem during the "seventh year" of the reign of Artaxerxes (in 458 BC).

8. The arrival of Nehemiah in Jerusalem in the "twentieth year" of Artaxerxes (in 445 BC). During his time in Jerusalem, which lasted more than a dozen years and involved at least two separate trips to Judea from Persia, Nehemiah rebuilt the walls of the city and instituted the lasting religious and moral reforms I have mentioned. The story of the building of the walls is told in chapters 1–7 of Nehemiah. The story of the religious reforms is told in chapters 8–13. They concern: (1) the instruction of the people (chaps. 8–10) and (2) the consolidation of the work (chaps. 11–13).[1]

First Things First

But this study is primarily about leadership, not history. So leaving the historical background behind, I ask this question: What makes a great leader? And since we want to become leaders ourselves: Where do we acquire the skills that characterize true leaders?

In one of Peter Drucker's books on leadership, there is a chapter entitled "First Things First." It concerns priorities, as one might suspect from its title, and it introduces what the author rightly calls one great "secret" of effectiveness: "Effective executives do first things first and they do one thing at a time."[2] This is a good principle, of course. In fact, it is two principles: (1) establishing priorities and (2) managing time effectively. But it raises these follow-up questions: What should the leader's priorities be? What things really are "first things"?

Some managers would put relationships with people first. Others would stress personal thought time, time for planning. These are important, but it is significant that when the problem of the broken walls of Jerusalem was presented to Nehemiah, the first priority of this great and (later) very successful leader was *prayer*. The first thing he did was unburden his heart to God, as we see at the close of the first chapter. Why do you suppose Nehemiah started here? There may be several reasons. For one thing, he was a man who prayed frequently about everything. Prayer was a habit for him, as we will see. But I suspect also that, in this case at least, Nehemiah prayed for the simple reason that no one but God could accomplish what needed to be accomplished if the walls of the city were to rise again.

Prayer made Abraham Lincoln the man he was, and for the same reason. He said on one occasion, "I have been driven many times to my knees by the overwhelming conviction that I had nowhere else to go. My own wisdom and that of those about me seemed insufficient for the day."[3]

Is this what makes a leader? The world may not think so, but the Bible teaches that this is the first and greatest dynamic: the leader and God.

The First Dynamic

We are going to be looking at Nehemiah's mastery of prayer more than once in this volume, but there is no better way to be introduced to it than by a study of the prayer with which the book starts. Here are three important aspects of it:

1. The attitude with which one should pray (v. 4). Nehemiah was an important man even before his success in rebuilding the walls of Jerusalem. Many important people are quite arrogant—arrogant with others and, I suppose, arrogant before God. But Nehemiah did not show this spirit. He was a man of courage and bold action, as we will see later on in the story. But here he humbles himself before God even to the point of tears and fasting. Nehemiah is not presumptuous, but he knows that God can do what he asks him to do. Therefore he comes submissively and seriously.

We need people who will pray like that today. Cyril J. Barber, the author of a very valuable study of Nehemiah, has written wisely, "The self-sufficient do not pray; they merely talk to themselves. The self-satisfied will not pray; they have no knowledge of their need. The self-righteous cannot pray; they have no basis on which to approach God."[4] A true leader is one who is not self-sufficient, self-satisfied, or self-righteous. On the contrary, he knows his need and is ready to humble himself before the One who alone is sufficient for it.

Great leaders are great prayer warriors.

2. The prayer itself (vv. 5–11). There is an acrostic for prayer that you have probably heard: ACTS. In this acrostic, *A* stands for adoration, *C* for confession, *T* for thanksgiving, and *S* for supplication. Each of these is present in Nehemiah's model prayer.

The first is *adoration*. It is expressed in this sentence: "O LORD, God of heaven, the great and awesome God, who keeps his covenant of love with those who love him and obey his commands, let your ear be attentive and your eyes open to hear the prayer your servant is praying before you day and night for your servants, the people of Israel" (vv. 5–6). This is a summary of Nehemiah's regular prayer worship, as is evident from his saying that he prayed like this "day and night." It is a short statement, but it acknowledges several great attributes of God: his sovereignty, love, faithfulness, and his ability to see and hear all that is going on, including Nehemiah's prayer.

Nehemiah does not proceed to the other elements of his prayer until he has reminded himself of what he is doing and the greatness and character of the God to whom he is directing his prayer.

The second element in Nehemiah's prayer is *confession of sin*. "I confess the sins we Israelites, including myself and my father's house, have committed against you. We have acted very wickedly toward you. We have not obeyed the commands, decrees and laws you gave your servant Moses" (vv. 6–7).

Nehemiah knew that the sin of the Israelites had caused the judgment of God that resulted in the destruction of Jerusalem. If Jerusalem were to be restored, it would need to be restored upon the basis of a confession of these sins. So Nehemiah is specific about them: "We have not obeyed the commands, decrees and laws you gave your servant Moses." What is most striking about his confession is that he includes himself in the acknowledgment of these sins: "the sins we Israelites, including myself and my father's house, have committed against you." There are two important principles here. First, Nehemiah recognizes the principle of solidarity—he is one with the people, so his sins are their sins and theirs are his. He does not try to distance himself from them. Second, Nehemiah recognizes that he is himself a sinner. There is no sin of the people that led to the fall of Jerusalem of which he is not guilty or is not capable of having done in the same circumstances.

Here is a secret of true leadership. A true leader is not so much aware of the talents or gifts he has that others do not have as he is of the fact that he is as weak and as capable of sin as anyone. It is when leaders forget their sinfulness that they fall into sin and lose their leadership ability.

The third element in this and all good prayers is *thanksgiving*. In this case it is expressed in Nehemiah's review of God's promises: "Remember the instruction you gave our servant Moses, saying, 'If you are unfaithful, I will scatter you among the nations, but if you return to me and obey my commands, then even if your exiled people are at the farthest horizon, I will gather them from there and bring them to the place I have chosen as a dwelling for my Name.' They are your servants and your people, whom you redeemed by your great strength and your mighty hand" (vv. 8–10).

These words are not an exact quotation of any one Old Testament passage, but they aptly express the great covenant principle of Deuteronomy, expressed most clearly in chapters 28 and 30. That covenant had two sides: (1) blessing and (2) judgment. It was conditional. If the people obeyed God, he would bless them and establish them securely in the land. But if they disobeyed him, he would scatter them, as he had done through the overthrow of the northern kingdom in 721 BC and the southern kingdom in 586 BC. Nehemiah reviews this promise because although it contains a warning of judgment following disobedience (which the people had experienced), it also suggests a time of blessing if the people should repent.

By his repentance, Nehemiah wants to represent the people in a way that will cause God to be merciful to them once again.

The fourth and final element in the ACTS acrostic is *supplication*, which Nehemiah employs as a conclusion to his prayer (v. 11). Having acknowledged God's greatness, confessed his own sin, and reviewed God's promises, he now lays his petitions before God: "O Lord, let your ear be attentive to the prayer of this your servant and to the prayer of your servants who delight in revering your name. Give your servant success today by granting him favor in the presence of this man" (v. 11).

"This man" was King Artaxerxes, whom Nehemiah introduces in the next verse, the first of chapter 2. He recognizes that the king is the key to the plan he is already developing and that God is the key to changing the king's heart.

Harry S. Truman, the thirty-second president of the United States, referred to leaders as "people who can get other people to do what they do not want to do—and make them like doing it." But if you have ever tried to get someone to do what he doesn't want to do and to like doing it, you know how difficult that is. I think even Dale Carnegie found it difficult. He knew it was important. He gave a sixth of his book *How to Win Friends and Influence People* to discussing "Nine Ways to Change People without Giving Offense or Causing Resentment." But of the many sections in the book this one is, in my judgment, the least satisfactory—obviously because the subject is so difficult.

How do you get people to change their minds? Generally you cannot, but God can, even in the case of kings. Proverbs 21:1 puts it in memorable language:

> The king's heart is in the hand of the LORD;
> he directs it like a watercourse wherever he pleases.

Hudson Taylor, founder of the China Inland Mission (now the Overseas Missionary Fellowship), knew this secret. He rightly states, "It is possible to move men through God by prayer alone."

3. Persistence in prayer (2:1). The final thing we need to see about Nehemiah's prayer life, the first of his great accomplishments as a leader, is his persistence. We know he was persistent in his prayers because of a detail linking the first verse of chapter 1 with the first verse of chapter 2. In chapter 1 Nehemiah says the delegation from Jerusalem came to him in the month of Kislev, which corresponds to a portion of our months of November/December. In chapter 2, when the king hears Nehemiah's request and grants permission for him to return to Jerusalem and rebuild its walls, it is the month of Nisan, which corresponds to our months of March/April. In other words, four or five months passed between the time Nehemiah began to petition God regarding Jerusalem and the time his requests were answered.

That is perseverance, a characteristic of all great leaders. Some leaders are great in persevering with men. Nehemiah was great in that area, but before he persevered with men he persevered with God, and prevailed.

"A Friend Is Come"

I close this chapter by reminding you of a New Testament story told by Jesus Christ. A man was at home one evening when a friend came to see him. He had nothing to give his friend after his journey, so he went to a neighbor and presented this request: "Friend, lend me three loaves of bread, because a friend of mine on a journey has come to me, and I have nothing to set before him." The neighbor was already in bed and did not want to be disturbed. "Don't bother me. . . . I can't get up and give you anything," he said. But the friend persisted, and finally the neighbor gave him what he needed.

Jesus concludes, "So I say to you: Ask and it will be given to you; seek and you will find; knock and the door will be opened to you. For everyone who asks receives; he who seeks finds; and to him who knocks, the door will be opened" (Luke 11:9–10; the parable is in vv. 5–10).

The part of that story that interests me most is the greeting from the friend to his neighbor: "Friend, a friend has come." That is a double friendship, you see. He was a friend to the man who had come to see him, the one who was in need. But he was also a friend to the man who had what was needed. Since this is a story about prayer, it shows that we must be on a friendship basis not only with other people but with God as well.

A leader is a people person. A leader sees the needs of others and grieves over them. Nehemiah saw the need and wept. But even more important than his tears was the fact that Nehemiah prayed. More important than his friendship with people was his friendship with God, since it is God alone who is able to change hearts, move kingdoms, and provide for our many needs.

2

The Second Dynamic:
The Leader and His Superiors

Nehemiah 2:1–8

In the month of Nisan in the twentieth year of King Artaxerxes, when wine was brought for him, I took the wine and gave it to the king. I had not been sad in his presence before; so the king asked me, "Why does your face look so sad when you are not ill? This can be nothing but sadness of heart."

I was very much afraid, but I said to the king, "May the king live forever! Why should my face not look sad when the city where my fathers are buried lies in ruins, and its gates have been destroyed by fire?"

The king said to me, "What is it you want?"

Then I prayed to the God of heaven, and I answered the king, "If it pleases the king and if your servant has found favor in his sight, let him send me to the city in Judah where my fathers are buried so that I can rebuild it."

Then the king, with the queen sitting beside him, asked me, "How long will your journey take, and when will you get back?" It pleased the king to send me; so I set a time.

I also said to him, "If it pleases the king, may I have letters to the governors of Trans-Euphrates, so that they will provide me safe-conduct until I arrive in Judah? And may I have a letter to Asaph, keeper of the king's forest, so he will give me timber to make beams for the gates of the citadel by the temple and for the city wall and for the residence I will occupy?" And because the gracious hand of my God was upon me, the king granted my requests.

Nehemiah 2:1–8

Wͤe saw in the last chapter that the first dynamic of effective leadership illustrated in the memoirs of Nehemiah, the governor of Jerusalem from 445 to 432 BC, is the relationship between the leader and God, the leader's ultimate superior. Unless his or her relationship to God is right, the leader will never be God's choice for any situation; nor in the final analysis will the leader ever be effective. Still, it is not only to a heavenly superior that leaders must relate. They must also relate to earthly ones, and for this reason the second dynamic for any true leader involves what we generally refer to as the role of middle management.

At the beginning of this story, Nehemiah was in a middle-management position, and the superior he reported to was Artaxerxes.

Problems of Middle Management

Middle management is a very important matter for two reasons: (1) most leaders are in middle-management positions, and (2) middle management is difficult.

Recently I have been talking with other people about middle-management positions in churches, particularly the role of executive pastors. An executive pastor is supposed to run a large church in order to free up the senior pastor. But he is not the senior pastor. He has to report to him. The position he finds himself in can become quite difficult. One very able executive pastor, who has since left that position to manage an inner-city seminary, told me that in his opinion, on the basis of his experience, an executive pastor's job is almost impossible to carry out. He is supposed to initiate and implement programs, but nobody considers that he has the real authority to do so. Instead of responding to him, the officers of the church generally look from him to the senior pastor to get the superior's response.

Similar problems occur in the business world. If a middle manager is alert, visionary, and innovative, he is frequently a threat to his boss—or his boss perceives this to be so. On the other hand, if he is merely an echo of his boss, he is of little value to him or to the organization.

How are middle managers to function? How can a person in this position be supportive and effective at the same time?

For anyone who is in this position, the second chapter of Nehemiah should be a great encouragement. Nehemiah was in a middle-management position, at least at the beginning of the story. Later, when he had been appointed governor of Jerusalem, technically he was still in middle management since his ultimate superior remained King Artaxerxes. Judah was still part of the great Persian Empire. But at that point Nehemiah was far removed from the palace—Jerusalem was fifteen hundred miles from Susa—and in most areas he could function entirely on his own authority. In chapter 2, by contrast, Nehemiah was attending on the king. There was nothing he could do—he could not even leave the city—without the king's permission.

Moreover, not only was Nehemiah in a middle-management position, but it was also an extremely trying one. He had no rights. The kings of Persia were absolute rulers. Their word was law.

And they were difficult.

Difficult? That is an understatement. The Persian kings were impossible at best and were often cruel. Since their oppressive policies were acutely resented by those they ruled, they were almost always in danger of assassination or revolt, so they were usually suspicious of any wrong moves or apparent lack of loyalty by their subordinates. We see a trace of this in Nehemiah 2:2, when the king notices that Nehemiah is sad and asks about it ("Why does your face look so sad when you are not ill? This can be nothing but sadness of heart"). Nehemiah was not overcome with gratitude that a person as important and busy as Artaxerxes should take notice of and be concerned for him. Rather, as he tells us, he "was very much afraid." He had a right to be. Persian rulers did not like subordinates to be gloomy in their presence.

Nehemiah's difficulties did not stop there. To be sad in King Artaxerxes' presence was dangerous enough. In addition to that, Nehemiah wanted to go to Jerusalem and rebuild its walls, and it was this king who earlier had been petitioned and had stopped work on the rebuilding of the walls as a result of that petition. Nehemiah's plan meant asking him to reverse his own policy.

In the last chapter, I mentioned the opposition to the first attempt to rebuild the walls, which took place under Ezra and was recorded by him. A strong Jerusalem was a threat to the supremacy of the nearby city-states, so when the second group of exiles returned under Ezra and began to rebuild the walls subsequent to their beginning to rebuild the temple, the rulers of the region of Trans-Euphrates petitioned Artaxerxes as follows:

To King Artaxerxes,

From your servants, the men of Trans-Euphrates:

The king should know that the Jews who came up to us from you have gone to Jerusalem and are rebuilding that rebellious and wicked city. They are restoring the walls and repairing the foundations. Furthermore, the king should know that if this city is built and its walls are restored, no more taxes, tribute, or duty will be paid, and the royal revenues will suffer. Now since we are under obligation to the palace and it is not proper for us to see the king dishonored, we are sending this message to inform the king, so that a search may be made in the archives of your predecessors. In these records you will find that this city is a rebellious city, troublesome to kings and provinces, a place of rebellion from ancient times. That is why this city was destroyed. We inform the king that if this city is built and its walls are restored, you will be left with nothing in Trans-Euphrates.

Ezra 4:11–16

After receiving a letter like that, it is no wonder Artaxerxes stopped the work. "Why let this threat grow, to the detriment of the royal interests?" he asked (v. 22). It was no small matter for Nehemiah to convince the king to reverse his own "wise" policy.

Success in Middle Management

Nehemiah succeeded, and his success shows how we too can succeed in middle management. Chapter 2 gives six secrets to Nehemiah's triumph.

1. Loyalty. The story does not make a great point of Nehemiah's loyalty to King Artaxerxes, but Nehemiah's whole demeanor as well as his success presupposes it. When the king asked why Nehemiah's face looked sad and he replied with the expected court greeting, "May the king live forever!" it was not hypocrisy or even mere formality. Nehemiah genuinely seems to have had the king's interests at heart.

Many persons in middle management err at just this point. Sometimes they err obviously and openly by trying to outshine the boss or to make him look bad. By doing so, they hope to advance over his failure. At other times they are not even aware of what they are doing, or they try to change the boss, expecting to correct his weaknesses rather than build on his strengths.

Peter Drucker says that the right sort of loyalty is to the advantage of the middle manager as well as his boss. "Contrary to popular legend, subordinates do not, as a rule, rise to position and prominence over the prostrate bodies of incompetent bosses. If their boss is not promoted, they will tend to be bottled up behind him. And if their boss is relieved for incompetence or failure, the successor is rarely the bright, young man next in line. He usually is brought in from the outside and brings with him his own bright, young men. Conversely, there is nothing quite as conducive to success, as a successful and rapidly promoted superior."[1]

This is not promoting a false or sinful loyalty, of course. To be loyal does not mean that we are to appear loyal when we are actually opposed to what is happening, or that we are loyally to support wrong actions. It merely means that as long as we are working for someone we must be loyal to him. If we cannot be loyal, we should seek employment elsewhere.

2. Tact. We speak about tact often, yet more often we fail to exercise it. We think it is more needful to "speak our minds," "express our frustrations," or "let it all hang out." Notice how tactful Nehemiah was with Artaxerxes.

First, when the king asked why he was sad, Nehemiah answered with a disarming question. Many of us would have said, "Why am I sad? I'll tell you why I'm sad. Thirteen years ago, in the seventh year of your reign, a delegation of Jews went to Jerusalem with the Jewish scribe Ezra. They tried to carry out the decree of your predecessor Cyrus to rebuild the temple and walls. But as soon as the governors of Trans-Euphrates heard about it and appealed to you to have the work stopped, you stopped it, and you didn't even wait to hear the other side of the story. You couldn't see that those governors were simply jealous of us and were afraid that a revitalized Jerusalem would be detrimental to their interests."

Many of us would have replied along those lines. But although our reply might have made us feel better, we would have experienced the failure such an arrogant attitude deserves. The king would have become defensive, and our cause would have been lost.

Instead of this, Nehemiah asked, "Why should my face not look sad when the city where my fathers are buried lies in ruins, and its gates have been destroyed by fire?" (v. 3). This question, instead of making Artaxerxes defensive, actually won him to Nehemiah's side. The king understood that Nehemiah had cause to be sad and wanted to help him.

Second, Nehemiah presented his desire as a personal matter and not as a political one. He knew that what he wanted would require the reversal of Artaxerxes' former public policy (Ezra 4:7–23), and he understood that any request to fortify a city was suspicious. So he did not treat this as a political issue at all. He treated it as a matter of personal grief, which the king, who was proud of his own city and who also had his own ancestors, would understand.

This is also the tack Esther took when she was asked to intercede with Artaxerxes' predecessor, King Xerxes. An official in the palace named Haman had formed an anti-Semitic plot according to which, on a certain day, all the Jews in the empire were to be killed and their possessions plundered. Mordecai, the uncle and guardian of Esther before her marriage to the king, heard of it and instructed Esther to intercede for the Jews, even at risk to her own life. What is significant here is that when she had a chance to implore Xerxes, she did not present the problem as a matter of civil wrong or injustice, which would have made the king defensive since he had (not knowing the full extent of or reason for the plot) given his sanction to it. Rather, she presented her cause personally.

Esther said, "If I have found favor with you, O King, and if it pleases your majesty, grant me my life—this is my petition. And spare my people—this is my request. For I and my people have been sold for destruction and slaughter and annihilation" (Esther 7:3–4). The king was astonished that anyone should have planned to destroy his wife. So, disregarding his own role in the policy, he reversed the decree, spared the Jews, and hanged Haman.

Third, it is worth noting, as many commentators have, that although Nehemiah asked for permission to rebuild the walls of Jerusalem, he nowhere actually mentioned Jerusalem by name. He referred to it as "the city where my fathers are buried" (v. 3) and "the city in Judah" (v. 5).

It is a simple point but a good one. As Dale Carnegie expressed it, "If you want to gather honey, don't kick over the beehive."[2]

3. Honesty. To be tactful does not mean that one is to be insincere. Nehemiah exhibited honesty in his encounter with the king in two ways.

First, when the king asks why Nehemiah is sad, he replies with two absolutely accurate statements, one directed to the reader (in the narrative) and the other to the king. To the reader he admits, "I was very much afraid" (v. 2). No false bravado here. To the king he replies that he is sad because the city of his fathers is in ruins (v. 3).

We know this is what was really bothering Nehemiah because in the chapter before this, when he was first told about the city's condition, Nehemiah "sat down and wept . . . mourned and fasted and prayed before the God of heaven" (Neh. 1:4). It is a wonder that he was able to keep his sadness hidden for so long. (There was a passing of four or five months between the time he heard the news and the time the king addressed him.) Nevertheless, when he was asked the reason for his sadness, he was honest. He did not try to invent a more acceptable reason for it.

Second, when the king asked what Nehemiah wanted, Nehemiah told him. He did not pretend that he wanted to take a vacation to Jerusalem or merely look the city over. From the first, he told the king he wanted to rebuild it.

This is very important. A good leader is willing to have those who work under him develop their own programs, but he does not want to be surprised by the plans of subordinates, and understandably so. Subordinates want their own plans to succeed, but the boss is responsible not only for the subordinate's plan but also for the success of the entire operation. He needs to know what is going on and to be able to approve, disapprove, or redirect those plans according to the larger picture.

Here is a secret: If you want to succeed with your boss, don't surprise him. Be creative, but be sure he is with you as you plow along.

4. Prayer. We have already looked at Nehemiah's great model prayer in chapter 1, noting that it had the elements of a formal petition: adoration, confession, thanksgiving, and supplication. It gives insight into Nehemiah's habits of personal devotion. Here we see something else. Nehemiah is talking to the king. The king asks what Nehemiah wants. He realizes that after months of prayer the decisive moment has arrived. He is ready to speak. But before he speaks, he utters a quick additional prayer to "the God of heaven" (v. 4).

One commentator calls this "a rapid heavenward plea."[3] Cyril Barber calls it a "prayergram."[4]

5. *Planning.* The most striking secret of middle-management success revealed in Nehemiah's encounter with King Artaxerxes is careful planning. To put it in simple language: (1) Nehemiah had a single fixed goal (he wanted to rebuild Jerusalem), and (2) he had worked out how he would achieve it.

Let me take those one at a time. First, Nehemiah had a goal. In the last study, when I was dealing with priorities, I quoted Peter Drucker's statement that "effective executives do first things first and they do one thing at a time."[5] I was speaking about prayer in that chapter, but the same principle of putting first things first applies to goal setting. We need to put first things first here also. But how can we do that unless we work out our goals carefully? It cannot be done, because unless a leader has a clear understanding of what he is trying to do and why it is important, other important but lesser matters will crowd in to chase the proper goals out.

Careful planning begins with goal setting. As one humorist has said, "People who aim at nothing are sure to hit it."

There is a story involving Yogi Berra, the well-known catcher for the New York Yankees, and Hank Aaron, who at that time was the chief power hitter for the Milwaukee Braves. The teams were playing in the World Series, and as usual Yogi was keeping up his ceaseless chatter, intended to pep up his teammates on the one hand and distract the Milwaukee batters on the other. As Aaron came to the plate, Yogi tried to distract him by saying, "Henry, you're holding the bat wrong. You're supposed to hold it so you can read the trademark." Aaron didn't say anything, but when the next pitch came he hit it into the left-field bleachers.

After rounding the bases and tagging up at home plate, Aaron looked at Yogi Berra and said, "I didn't come up here to read." He knew his goal, and he did not allow Berra to distract him.

The second part of planning involves ways to achieve the fixed goal. It had been four or five months since Nehemiah had begun to pray about how he might rebuild Jerusalem, but he had not been inactive during those months. First, he gathered information. As his requests to Artaxerxes unfold, we are impressed by his knowledge of the area to which he is going, even to knowing the name of Asaph, the keeper of the king's forest. Second, he had worked out what he would need to get the walls built. He was specific: (1) he knew how long it would take (twelve years, cf. Neh. 5:14; 13:6);[6] (2) he needed letters of safe-conduct for the governors of the Trans-Euphrates region; and (3) he asked for requisitions of the supplies that would be needed.

When his opportunity came, Nehemiah was ready. He said, "If it pleases the king, may I have letters to the governors of Trans-Euphrates, so that they will provide me safe-conduct until I arrive in Judah? And may I have a letter to Asaph, keeper of the king's forest, so he will give me timber to make beams for the gates of the citadel by the temple and for the city wall and for the residence I will occupy?" (Neh. 2:7–8).

Careful planning! If he had not thought the matter through carefully, his conversation with the king might have ended with permission for him to go to Jerusalem, but he would have been stopped by the governors of Trans-Euphrates. If he had asked for letters of passage and had therefore been able to get to his destination but had neglected to secure the requisitions, he would have arrived without being able to obtain the necessary materials.

It is surprising how often careful planning is overlooked by persons in leadership, whether in the church or outside it in business or government. In Christian circles, the problem may be traceable to a false spirituality that goes like this:

"God has told me to do so and so," the dreamer says.

"Yes? And how are you going to do it?"

"I don't know. I guess I'm just going to start out and see what the Lord does for me." People who start this way usually return with the job not finished.

Counting the cost is crucial before we commit ourselves to any task. Jesus said:

> Suppose one of you wants to built a tower. Will he not first sit down and estimate the cost to see if he has enough money to complete it? For if he lays the foundation and is not able to finish it, everyone who sees it will ridicule him, saying, "This fellow bgan to build and was not able to finish."
>
> Or suppose a king is about to go to war against another king. Will he not first sit down and consider whether he is able with ten thousand men to oppose the one coming against him with twenty thousand? If he is not able, he will send a delegation while the other is still a long way off and will ask for terms of peace. In the same way, any of you who does not give up everything he has cannot be my disciple.
>
> Luke 14:28–33

6. Dependence on God. Dependence on God does not eliminate planning any more than it eliminates hard work. But while Nehemiah was planning, he was also praying. After the king had granted his request to go to Jerusalem to rebuild the walls and had agreed to supply him with the necessary letters of requisition, Nehemiah acknowledged that in the final analysis his success was not due to his own careful planning but to God: "And because the gracious hand of my God was upon me, the king granted my requests" (v. 8).

Isn't that wonderful? Nehemiah had done everything he possibly could, but when he achieved success he acknowledged that it had come about not because of his wisdom but because God had been with him.

This is the difference between a Christian and a secular view of history. The secularist says, "But surely there were other factors that disposed the powerful Persian monarch in his favor." No doubt there were. There had been a revolt in lower Egypt in the late 460s BC, encouraged by the Greeks of Athens. Then, in the 440s, there had been a rebellion in Syria. Persian forces had crushed both these rebellions, but pockets of resistance still remained and the region was unstable. At this point in history, Artaxerxes may have reasoned that a stronger Judah populated by loyal Jews would strengthen his position in the west and be a buffer against Egypt.[7] Because of his position, Nehemiah might even have known of this plan and conducted himself accordingly.

But Nehemiah did not thank man for the favorable outcome to his request. Man had acted, but it was God who had directed events and steered the heart of Artaxerxes.

Artaxerxes' Favorable Response

The climax of this encounter came in Artaxerxes' granting his cupbearer's requests. Not only did he grant them, but also he seems to have exceeded what Nehemiah asked for since he also sent army officers and cavalry along with him. These must have impressed the governors of Trans-Euphrates greatly, not to mention the Jews of Jerusalem.

God will provide beyond what we ask him for too. Haven't you found that to be the case? It is true that God does not always answer our prayers when or how we expect him to. There are willful, stubborn prayers that we should not even be praying. He will not answer them at all—except to say no. But when we pray in God's will and wait on him to answer in his own time, we find that what God does is perfect—it is that "good, pleasing and perfect will" Paul writes of in Romans 12:2—and that it is beyond our expectations. As Paul also says, God "is able to do immeasurably more than all we ask or imagine, according to his power that is at work within us" (Eph. 3:20).

3

The Third Dynamic: Taking Command

Nehemiah 2:9–20

I went to Jerusalem, and after staying there three days I set out during the night with a few men. I had not told anyone what my God had put in my heart to do for Jerusalem. There were no mounts with me except the one I was riding on.

By night I went out through the Valley Gate toward the Jackal Well and the Dung Gate, examining the walls of Jerusalem, which had been broken down, and its gates, which had been destroyed by fire. Then I moved on toward the Fountain Gate and the King's Pool, but there was not enough room for my mount to get through; so I went up the valley by night, examining the wall. Finally, I turned back and reentered through the Valley Gate. The officials did not know where I had gone or what I was doing, because as yet I had said nothing to the Jews or the priests or nobles or officials or any others who would be doing the work.

Then I said to them, "You see the trouble we are in: Jerusalem lies in ruins, and its gates have been burned with fire. Come, let us rebuild the wall of Jerusalem, and we will no longer be in disgrace." I also told them about the gracious hand of my God upon me and what the king had said to me.

They replied, "Let us start rebuilding." So they began this good work.

Nehemiah 2:11–18

31

One of the complaints raised against the Bible is that it is impractical and too "spiritual" to be of real use. The opinion is usually voiced by those who do not know the Bible well, though in fairness to their view it is right to acknowledge that the Bible does have spiritual goals. Even Nehemiah, which is extremely practical, has doctrinal themes. Howard F. Vos finds seven great teachings in Nehemiah: (1) God's providential care of his dispossessed people, (2) the fulfillment of prophecy, (3) how to handle opposition to the work of God, (4) prayer, (5) the importance of holiness, (6) the qualifications of God's servants, and (7) how to worship God.[1] But even these "spiritual" matters are presented practically, and as I have been pointing out, there is outstanding teaching about the very practical matter of leadership.

We have studied two of the dynamics of leadership: the relationship of the leader to God and the relationship of the leader to his superior or superiors. In this study we will look at the relationship of the leader to his subordinates seen in Nehemiah's account of his arrival in Jerusalem and the manner in which he took command.

An Overwhelming Problem

In one sense, Nehemiah is the story of a great man meeting and overcoming challenges. We have already seen how he met the challenge of persuading King Artaxerxes to send him to Jerusalem. It was difficult because Persian kings could not easily be persuaded to do anything and because, in this case, the request involved getting Artaxerxes to reverse a previously established policy. Nehemiah succeeded with this first challenge, but now that he had arrived in Jerusalem, he faced a second problem that was no less difficult.

The problem was to get the wall of Jerusalem built. These were the difficulties:

1. *The task was overwhelming.* Commentators differ over the size of the city at this time and therefore over the length of wall Nehemiah was to build. But even by the most modest estimates, the circumference of the city was one and a half to two and a half miles.[2] Moreover, the destruction was great, and the stones to be reassembled were massive. This was not a case of a group of workers merely constructing a garden fence, a brick wall, or even a large earthwork fortification. The blocks that had been tumbled down into the valleys below were of great weight, and these had to be exposed and then hauled back up to the site of the wall and reassembled. This required many workers, diverse skills, and even, we may suppose, a certain amount of lifting and moving machinery.

2. *A history of defeat.* Nehemiah faced a second great difficulty. Not only was the task itself overwhelming, but it also had been attempted before and had been given up, which meant he was bucking a history of defeat.

Nehemiah arrived in Jerusalem in the twentieth year of King Artaxerxes, which was 445 BC, but the work had actually begun in the second year of King Cyrus in 538 BC, more than ninety years earlier. At the time, the first contingent of Jews tried to rebuild the temple, but even that lesser task had proved difficult. It took fifteen years to get the temple finished. Then, when the first attempt to reerect the walls was made, opposition arose and the appeal by the governors of Trans-Euphrates to Artaxerxes to have the building stopped was successful. This happened after the return of a second wave of exiles in the seventh year of Artaxerxes. When Nehemiah arrived, the most recent failure was only thirteen years in the past. Nehemiah faced not only a difficult task but inertia as well.

3. A discouraged group of workers. To make matters worse, the only people Nehemiah had to work with were discouraged—as we also would have been in that situation. If Nehemiah had approached the matter without careful preparation, they would have said, "We cannot do it. We have tried several times already and have failed each time. We cannot change the situation."

An overwhelming task? Yes. But overwhelming tasks are opportunities for great men, which Nehemiah was. In chapter 2:11–18, turning from his superior to his subordinates, we see how he went about changing the situation so that within the next fifty-two days (less than two months), this great task was accomplished. As in the case of his dealings with King Artaxerxes, when Nehemiah was in a position of middle management, we see six elements to his success.

Planning for Success

First, Nehemiah was a great planner—a prayer *and* a planner. He knew, as we should know also, that the two are not opposed to each other but rather support one another. Before he spoke to the king about wanting to go to Jerusalem, Nehemiah formulated a plan for how he could accomplish his goal. Here, in the second chapter we find him doing exactly the same thing, only now he is on the site, and the plan needs to be more specific.

What are the steps in producing a good plan?

1. Information. One of the best-known incidents in the book of Nehemiah is the one in which Nehemiah rides out by night to inspect the wall of the sleeping city. There are many things we might expect Nehemiah to do when he first arrives in Jerusalem—perhaps make a great show of arriving and assuming power, perhaps hold private interviews with the chief men of the city, maybe even try to set up alliances with the leaders of the cities round-about. We are therefore somewhat surprised that he does none of these things. In fact, for the first three days he does nothing. Then, on the third day, at night he takes a few trusted men and sets out on an examination of the walls. He is so detailed in his account that even today this (along with chap. 3) is the best historical record of the extent of the city in the postexilic period.

Nehemiah rode around the outside of the overthrown walls beginning with the Valley Gate, which was to the west of the city.

At this time, Jerusalem was located on two hills that ran parallel to each other from north to south and that were steepest on the west, south, and east. When Nehemiah exited by the Valley Gate, he was starting on the west at a point where the hills were quite steep. Once outside the gate, he turned south and proceeded past the Jackal Well to the Dung Gate, which was on the very south. As the name implies, the Dung Gate was the gate through which the refuse of the city was carried out of the populated area to the Valley of Hinnom. The Fountain Gate was a little farther along, at the southeastern corner of the city where the Hinnom and Kidron valleys met. The King's Pool is known to us as the Pool of Siloam. It is where Jesus told the blind man to wash (John 9:7). It was called the King's Pool as well as the Pool of Siloam because Hezekiah had built a tunnel from inside the wall to the pool, which was outside, to assure a supply of water in case of siege. On the west of the city were steep terraces so that when the wall was knocked down the stones fell into an impassable jumble. This is where Nehemiah dismounted, since his mount was unable to get through.[3]

Those who were accompanying Nehemiah were seeing nothing new, but he was. He was gathering the information necessary to plan the walls' reconstruction.

2. Conceptualization. After gathering the necessary information, Nehemiah developed a concept for how the rebuilding could be done. We are not told about it in chapter 2, but we know he developed it because as soon as he presented the people with his challenge to rebuild the wall (chap. 2), he was ready to move forward with it (chap. 3).

A person might wonder if, after one nighttime inspection of the damaged walls, Nehemiah could possibly have acquired all the information necessary for rebuilding them. The answer probably is no. Most likely he did not have *all* the information he was going to need before the task was finished. But the point is important, for this reason: although Nehemiah probably did not have all the information he needed to complete the rebuilding, he had enough to have formulated a sound, workable plan for doing it.

Managers need to learn this because many of them, afraid to make decisions, keep gathering information ("just to be sure that what we are doing is right") long after the opportunity to make a good decision has passed by.

When Robert McNamara was the United States secretary of defense under John Kennedy, he developed a procedure of acting on the information necessary to make a decision without trying to gather all the information, since "all information" can never be attained. For example, in trying to improve the procurement and inventory problems of the armed services, which had been in bad shape since the Korean War, McNamara abandoned the procedure of trying to make judgments on all military items and instead identified those few items, perhaps 4 percent, that together accounted for more than 90 percent of the expenditures. He managed these with minute attention to detail, and the result was a series of efficient procurement and inventory judgments.[4]

To have a workable plan, it is not necessary to have *all* information, but it is necessary to have the *necessary* information and then formulate a wise plan with it. Nehemiah did this before he spoke to the people of Jerusalem.

3. Implementation. There is one more aspect of producing a good plan that is often overlooked, mainly, I suppose, because we do not think of it as a part of good planning. It is what Robert J. Schoenberg calls a plan to implement the prior workable plan psychologically.[5] This means planning how one is going to get the people who will do it to respond. It involves knowing how to motivate one's subordinates effectively. Again, we are not told that psychological planning was part of Nehemiah's thought processes at this time, but we know it was because of the way he handles himself in the remainder of the chapter.

Arnold Toynbee, the great English historian, said, "Apathy can only be overcome by enthusiasm, and enthusiasm can only be aroused by two things: first, an ideal which takes the imagination by storm, and second, a definite intelligible plan for carrying that ideal into practice."[6] Nehemiah was confronted by a situation filled with apathy, and his first step was to formulate a plan to carry out his vision.

Timing Is (Almost) Everything

The second step was timing. In humor, as every really funny person knows, timing is everything. A punch line badly timed ruins the joke, while a line rightly timed makes it. Jack Benny was a master of timing, as in the famous routine in which he was confronted by a robber. "Your money or your life," the thief demanded.

Benny, who had a stage reputation for being tight with his money, paused a long time. People were already laughing.

"Well," said the robber.

"I'm thinking, I'm thinking," said Benny.

In a list of leadership skills, timing may not quite be everything, as it is in comedy, but it is important. Nehemiah seems to have been aware of this fact. That is why I list Nehemiah's timing as the second secret of his amazing success in managing and motivating his subordinates. We see it in several ways. On the one hand, we see it in his three-day time-out after his arrival in Jerusalem. If he had acted too quickly, without gathering the necessary facts, his ideas would have been dismissed as the uninformed and impractical daydreams of a novice. On the other hand, we see it in the prompt presentation of his plan to the people on the fourth day. If he had delayed longer, he would have lost the initiative that his prestige as the newly appointed governor gave him. By the end of the three days, his presence had aroused considerable curiosity. It was the moment to tell why he had left Susa for the fifteen-hundred-mile trip to Jerusalem.

"Come, Let Us Rebuild the Wall"

The third step in Nehemiah's plan was a direct challenge to the citizens. Verse 17 records what he said to "them." Since the immediate antecedent to this pronoun can only be what is in verse 16 ("the Jews . . . the priests . . . nobles . . . officials or any others who would be doing the work"), Nehemiah must have addressed them all, which he could have done only by calling a large convocation. The advantage of this was that he thereby had an opportunity to speak to each one directly. Each one got to hear him and make up his or her own mind about the challenge. No one had an opportunity to interpret (or misinterpret) his words to the others.

Dale Carnegie tells of a mill manager whose men were not producing. The owner, whose name was Charles Schwab, asked why. The manager had no idea. "I've coaxed the men; I've pushed them; I've sworn and cussed; I've threatened them with damnation and being fired. But nothing works. They just won't produce."

"How many heats did your shift make today?" Schwab asked.

"Six."

Without saying another word, Schwab picked up a piece of chalk and wrote a big figure 6 on the floor. Then he walked away.

When the night shift came in, they saw the 6 and asked what it meant. "The big boss was here today," someone said. "He asked how many heats the day shift made, and we told him six. He chalked it on the floor."

The next morning Schwab walked through the mill again. The night shift had rubbed out the 6 and replaced it with an even bigger 7. When the day shift reported the next day, they saw the 7. So the night shift thought it was better than the day shift, did it? They'd show them. They pitched in furiously, and before they had left that evening they had rubbed out the 7 and replaced it with a 10. It was a 66 percent increase in just twenty-four hours, and all because of Schwab's challenge.

Carnegie concludes, "If you want to win . . . spirited men . . . to your way of thinking . . . throw down a challenge."[7]

"We Can Make It Together"

The fourth secret of Nehemiah's success in getting the people of Jerusalem to support his plan was his identification with them in the task. Even though we have only a brief record of what Nehemiah said on this occasion, his identification with the people in the effort is striking. Notice the personal pronouns *we* and *us*. "You see the trouble *we* are in: Jerusalem lies in ruins, and its gates have been burned with fire. Come, let *us* rebuild the wall of Jerusalem, and *we* will no longer be in disgrace" (v. 17, italics added). If he had said, "You see what trouble *you* are in; *you* need to rebuild the wall," he would have gotten nowhere.

It is amazing what the equal participation of a leader can do to build morale. John R. Noe, president of IMH Systems in Indianapolis, a mountain climber, and a popular public speaker, tells of his first attempt to climb the Matterhorn on the Swiss-Italian border. He had prepared carefully, practicing on other mountains. Nevertheless, when he got to Zermatt, where the Matterhorn climb would commence, he had to pass the inspection of his hired Swiss guide and was nervous about it. The guide took him up the Riffelhorn, the qualifying peak for the Matterhorn. They climbed all day, going up and down this lesser mountain. Finally, in the late afternoon, the guide called a halt, loosened the rope from Noe's waist, and said slowly, "Well, John, it's going to be difficult for you, but I think *we* can make it *together*."[8]

It was that "we" and doing it "together" that inspired confidence.

"Blood, Toil, Tears, and Sweat"

In his study of these verses, Charles Swindoll distinguishes between external motivation, which Nehemiah did not use, and internal means, which he did. Most managers use external means exclusively, even though studies show that this is generally least effective. They think people are motivated primarily by money. Harvey S. Firestone, founder of the Firestone Tire and Rubber Company, said, "I have never found that pay and pay alone would either bring together or hold good men. I think it [is] the game itself."[9]

Take Winston Churchill as an example. He was a superb motivator, yet he seems never to have promised anything external—not prosperity, not leisure, not the return of good times. He offered only the satisfaction of having done the difficult task well. Churchill said:

> I have nothing to offer but blood, toil, tears, and sweat.
>
> What is our aim? I can answer in one word: Victory—victory at all costs, victory in spite of all terror; victory however long and hard the road may be; for without victory there is no survival.
>
> We shall not flag or fail. We shall go on to the end, we shall fight in France, we shall fight in the seas and oceans, we shall fight with growing confidence and growing strength in the air; we shall defend our island, whatever the cost may be, we shall fight on the beaches, we shall fight on the landing-grounds, we shall fight in the fields and in the streets, we shall fight in the hills; we shall never surrender, and even if, which I do not for a moment believe, this island

or a large part of it were subjugated and starving, then our Empire beyond the seas, armed and guarded by the British Fleet, would carry on the struggle, until, in God's good time, the New World, with all its power and might, steps forth to the rescue and the liberation of the old.[10]

Nehemiah's appeal was similar, though couched in less dramatic language. He challenged the people to rebuild so that "we will no longer be in disgrace" (v. 17). It was an appeal to their nobler instinct or patriotism.

Let me apply this spiritually. The people of Jerusalem were motivated by their earthly citizenship and responded, as the story shows, by rebuilding the walls of their city. We have a heavenly citizenship (Phil. 3:20). Are we proud of that citizenship? Are we motivated to work enthusiastically for the realization of God's kingdom here? There is work to be done, walls to be rebuilt. Besides, in contrast to the mere earthly building of Nehemiah's days, what we are to build—truth, character, and good deeds—is lasting.

John Newton, former slave trader, never lost the joy of being part of the heavenly enterprise. Perhaps that is why he wrote the following:

> Savior, if of Zion's city
> I through grace a member am.
> Let the world deride or pity,
> I will glory in thy name;
> Fading is the worldling's pleasure,
> All his boasted pomp and show;
> Solid joys and lasting treasure,
> None but Zion's children know.

Keep Other People Informed

The final secret of Nehemiah's success in arousing the people to rebuild the walls was his skills in taking them into his confidence. He kept them informed of the progress already attained. First, there had been a victory at the highest level: the king had altered his policy to permit the rebuilding. Second, God was behind the great project. Nehemiah reports, "I also told them about the gracious hand of my God upon me and what the king had said to me" (v. 18). If you are trying to lead others, don't forget this element. Keep people informed of what is happening. It is said of Martin Luther that one reason he was successful in leading the Reformation was that he kept the German people informed of what was happening and what he was doing at each stage.

"So They Began the Good Work"

In the earlier part of this chapter, after his conversation with King Artaxerxes, Nehemiah reported, "It pleased the king to send me" (v. 6) and

"The king granted my requests" (v. 8). This section ends similarly: "So they began this good work" (v. 18). Simple yet significant! There was much to do; there would be problems yet. But the work was under way.

Notice the word *good.* J. G. McConville, in his study *Ezra, Nehemiah, and Esther,* has a wonderful section in which he comments on the use of "evil" and "good" in this chapter. It is hidden in most English translations. But we should note the following: When Nehemiah's face is said to be "sad" in verses 1–3, the Hebrew word is actually *rà*, which means "evil." The same word is used when Nehemiah directs the people's attention to the "trouble" of Jerusalem (v. 17; see also 1:3). By contrast, when we are told that Nehemiah's request "pleased" the king (vv. 6–7), the word is *tov,* which means "good." The sentence literally says, "It was good to the king." Verses 8 and 18 literally say, "The good hand of my God was upon me." Finally, "so they began this good work." McConville writes:

> Underlying the action in this chapter, therefore, is a conflict between good and evil. Everything that serves the interests of the returned exiles—the king's decision, the rebuilding of the walls—is good; all that tends towards, or is the product of, their loss—the broken walls, Nehemiah's grief, the aspirations of Sanballat, Tobia, and Geshem—is evil. The clear implication of verse 10 is that the opposition to Judah from these powerful leaders is a spiritual thing.[11]

That is profoundly true, and it is no less true for us. If you are trying to serve God faithfully, then you are also engaged in spiritual warfare (cf. Eph. 6:10–18). Everything that tends to your victory is good. Everything that tends to your defeat is evil. If you can see that, it will make a great difference in how you fight the battle.

4

The Fourth Dynamic: How the Work Was Done

Nehemiah 3:1-32

Eliashib the high priest and his fellow priests went to work and rebuilt the Sheep Gate. . . . The men of Jericho built the adjoining section, and Zaccur son of Imri built next to them.

The Fish Gate was rebuilt by the sons of Hassenaah. . . .

The Jeshanah Gate was repaired by Joiada son of Paseah and Meshullam son of Besodeiah. . . . Uzziel son of Harhaiah, one of the goldsmiths, repaired the next section; and Hananiah, one of the perfume-makers, made repairs next to that. They restored Jerusalem as far as the Broad Wall. . . . Shallum son of Hallohesh, ruler of a half-district of Jerusalem, repaired the next section with the help of his daughters.

The Valley Gate was repaired by Hanun and the residents of Zanoah. . . .

The Dung Gate was repaired by Malkijah son of Recab, ruler of the district of Beth Hakkerem. . . .

The Fountain Gate was repaired by Shallun son of Col-Hozeh. . . . He also repaired the wall of the Pool of Siloam. . . .

Next to him . . . Next to him . . . Next to him . . .

Meshullam son of Berekiah made repairs opposite his living quarters. Next to him, Malkijah, one of the goldsmiths, made repairs as far as the house of the temple servants and the merchants, opposite the Inspection Gate, and as far as the room above the corner;

and between the room above the corner and the Sheep Gate the goldsmiths and merchants made repairs.

Nehemiah 3:1–3, 6, 8, 12–15, 17–19, 30–32

Τhe third chapter of Nehemiah is a detailed account of the way the gates and walls of the city Jerusalem were rebuilt, focusing on the names of those who were involved in the construction. Can anything be more uninteresting than a list of names, particularly names most of us can hardly pronounce?

Many people seem to think so, and not only laypeople. Charles Swindoll, in his otherwise excellent study of Nehemiah, *Hand Me Another Brick*, skips the chapter entirely, moving from Nehemiah's challenge to the people to rebuild the walls (in chap. 2) to the opposition that inevitably comes (in chap. 4). What I hope to show in this chapter is that Nehemiah 3 is actually one of the most important sections of the book and that it is even interesting. When it is properly understood, it is seen as a record of a most remarkable achievement. Here is what Howard F. Vos writes about it:

> What appears here at first blush to be a list of forgotten names and boring details of wall construction, on closer examination becomes something quite dramatic and exciting. It may be observed first, that what occurred was the result of an incredible feat of organization. The entire community was mobilized and was led to work harmoniously and simultaneously on all parts of the city wall, which was divided into forty or forty-one sections. Second, the entire work force demonstrated an unquenchable dedication and an ardent enthusiasm as they strained feverishly to complete the task. Third, it is clear that Julius Caesar, who was to come centuries later, had no monopoly on the tactics of speed and surprise, for which he is justly famous. The enemies of the Jews were completely caught off guard by the speed and drive of Nehemiah and his compatriots. Before they could effectively organize to stop the Jews or destroy their work, the walls and gates were restored. Fourth, this section of Nehemiah is also interesting because it is one of the best sources on the topography of ancient Jerusalem. Fifth, the passage shows the involvement of the whole Jewish community, as is demonstrated by the mention of representatives of crafts, trades, towns, and various social classes.[1]

The chapter is easy to analyze. It is constructed around seven gates of the city, moving in a counterclockwise direction, beginning with the Sheep Gate on the north side of the city next to the temple enclosure and eventually returning to it (cf. vv. 1, 32). A paragraph or a group of several paragraphs is devoted to the repair of each of these sections.

A Motivator and a Task Specialist

In the last chapter, I quoted a statement about apathy by English historian Arnold Toynbee: "Apathy can only be overcome by enthusiasm, and enthusiasm can only be aroused by two things: first, an ideal which takes the imagination by storm, and second, a definite intelligible plan for carrying that ideal into practice."[2] That "definite intelligible plan" was developed in the time period described in chapter 2, but in chapter 3 we see it unfolding.

What does this tell us about Nehemiah? He recognized the importance of a detailed plan, which means that in this chapter we have a fourth great dynamic of effective leadership. We have looked at three great dynamics already. The first is the relationship of the leader to God. This is sometimes overlooked even by Christians—secular leaders ignore it entirely—yet it is critical. I referred to it as putting first things first. The second dynamic is the relationship of the leader to his earthly superior or superiors. God is the ultimate superior, of course. But there are few people who do not have an earthly superior or superiors as well. It is important to know how to work creatively and well with such persons. The third dynamic is the relationship of the leader to those who are under him and for whose work he or she is responsible. This involves setting clear and communicable goals and providing motivation. Nehemiah also excelled in this area, even though he was dealing with a discouraged people who had a history of defeat.

But it is not only people with whom the effective leader must deal. There is also the work itself, and this, as I have already pointed out, is the fourth great dynamic. To put this in modern management jargon, Nehemiah needed to be not only a motivator but a task specialist as well. The task specialist is one who gets the work done.

How did Nehemiah do it? An examination of this chapter uncovers several important principles.

Manageable Sections

The most striking thing about Nehemiah 3, in my opinion, is something I have not seen specifically mentioned by any of the other writers on Nehemiah, except possibly Howard Vos: the fact that Nehemiah divided the work into manageable sections. I suppose the reason for the omission is that the point is so obvious. But obvious or not, it is critical. If the rebuilding of the walls had been tackled as a task whole in itself and if one person or even a group of people had been assigned to it, the work would have seemed impossible, and rightly so. Who could rebuild an entire mile-and-one-half or two-and-one-half-mile wall? Nobody. But when the project was divided into forty or forty-one separate segments, as the chapter shows it was, then that two-and-a-half-mile project became manageable.

Most managers know how to subdivide projects, of course, so this is perhaps a superfluous point for them. But there are lots of people who do not know how to manage projects. When faced with a large assignment, most people make one or more of these mistakes:

1. *Underestimating the task.* Sometimes this is due simply to lack of experience. They have never before faced something of the scope of the task, and they really do not know how much energy or skill it will take, or how long it will take, to complete it. At other times, this is due to an unwillingness to face up to a task perceived to be unpleasant. A student putting off studying for a final exam might be in this category. "There's plenty of time to study up," he might say. He actually needs all the time he can get. The reason the student speaks that way is that he or she does not want to face studying. The student needs to divide up the unpleasant work and then tackle a bit of it every day.

2. *Letting the work go until the end.* The student I have mentioned could also be an example of this second failure. He could simply be procrastinating, letting the work slide until it becomes too late to get it done.

3. *Spending time on later, more interesting problems before tackling earlier and more basic ones.* This is a natural tendency. If you like to plan parties rather than write letters, you might neglect to send out the invitations. Yet without the invitations there will be no parties. On one occasion, theologian Carl F. H. Henry was invited to a northwestern university to give lectures on Christianity. His host was an energetic young man named Doug Coe, who has since done marvelous work among government leaders in our nation's capital. Coe had a vision for reaching the university. He put together a planning committee, chose a theme, contacted his speaker, picked a date, and reserved the hall. But when the day came and Henry and Coe were together backstage before the first lecture, Coe looked out through the curtain and was stunned. There was no one there. Why? He had forgotten to advertise the event. So instead of the great meetings he had envisioned, his committee held a small Bible study with Henry presiding.

Dividing up the task (if it is well done) assures that each necessary part will get covered, the less exciting parts as well as those that are more challenging.

4. *Trying to do too many things at once.* Some people make the mistake of trying to do too many things at once or trying to do all that needs to be done themselves.

The proper way to get an important job done is the way Nehemiah went about it. The first step in his handling of the job was to divide it into manageable sections. There are two more things that should be said at this point. First, in most cases, what needs to follow the dividing of the task is prioritizing. Fundamental things need to be set in the first position. Lesser or more complex tasks need to be set further along. Second, again in most cases, these manageable sections need to be tackled one item at a time. Remember

Peter Drucker's comment: "Effective executives do first things first and they do one thing at a time."[3]

This involves time management, of course. It means that the effective leader must use time to his advantage.

I have found that one secret of managing my time well is blocking it so that I have sufficient time *at one time* to accomplish something, then fitting other things in around that. In a normal week my schedule looks something like this:

Monday: My day off. I usually spend it at home reading or doing projects I have not been able to do throughout the week.

Tuesday: A staff day. The morning is spent at Evangelical Ministries, the parent organization of *The Bible Study Hour.* In the afternoon I meet with members of the Tenth Presbyterian Church staff and catch up on administrative matters remaining from the weekend.

Wednesday: Creative time. I start early in the morning and use the bulk of the day preparing the message for the coming Sunday evening.

Thursday: A catchall day. In the morning I complete the work begun the day before. In the afternoon I meet with the ministerial staff and later with the total staff of the church.

Friday: Administration.

Saturday: Another sermon day. I use this day to write the Sunday morning message and do other Sunday preparation.

Sunday: Church work from beginning to end.

Into this general framework I fit other things. Some evenings are taken up with meetings: trustees, the session, various boards and committees. I use free evenings to read or to be with my wife and family. The church has a pastor who does visitation, so I do not typically do so. But there is some visiting to do, and I usually fit that into free evenings. I have a reasonable amount of counseling and appointments also. Generally I fit those in from the end of the day forward to preserve as much free morning time as possible.

Prioritizing! Doing one thing at a time! You may remember that when I mentioned these in connection with Nehemiah, I said "in most cases." This is because in Nehemiah's case, dividing the reconstruction of the wall into manageable sections did not result in one section being given priority over another or one section being completed before a second section was begun. In this case, the wall itself was the priority. The whole thing needed to be done as soon as possible—before the enemies of the Jews attacked them or in some other way hindered its completion. As we go on, however, we will see that Nehemiah had other goals too, and he worked on these at the appropriate time.

To Each a Task

The second striking but obvious thing about Nehemiah's approach to the work of rebuilding the walls is that he assigned different teams of people to each part. First, he divided the project into sections. Second, he made his assignments. This is what the chapter is primarily about. It is a list of those who rebuilt the gates and each adjoining section of the walls.

I want you to see several important points:

1. Nehemiah delegated the authority. Nothing in the chapter makes a specific point of this, but it is obvious that this is what happened. Nehemiah made the assignments, but from then on he seems to have allowed each group of workers to proceed as it saw fit. This is clear from the slight variations in how the work was done. Is delegation important? Robert Townsend, author of *Up the Organization* and *Further Up the Organization*, thinks it is. Further, he thinks it is important to delegate even the most important matters. He writes:

> A real leader does as much of the dog work for this people as he can: he can do it, or see a way to do without it, ten times as fast. And he delegates as many important matters as he can because that creates a climate in which people grow. . . . Make sure the jobs you give your people are *whole* and *important* and that you really give them the jobs. Ask them not to report unless they're in trouble. Grit your teeth and don't ask them how it's going.[4]

2. Nehemiah got everyone involved. It is amazing to see the number and the various types of people involved in rebuilding these walls. The names of forty-one heads of task-force groups are mentioned, and that does not include the names of places (from which others came) or the names of the individuals' fathers or grandfathers (who may have been working also). Think of the types of workers. Cyril J. Barber calls attention to "priests and Levites, rulers and common people, gatekeepers and guards, farmers and 'union men'—goldsmiths, pharmacists, merchants—temple servants and women."[5] It is worth looking at some of these as they occur in the chapter.

Priests. The priests must have played an important part. They are listed first, verse 1 speaking of "Eliashib the high priest and his fellow priests." They are also mentioned near the end (v. 28), after the narrative has made its way back around the walls to the point of origin. Priests are listed along the way too. Verse 17 speaks of "the Levites [who were priests] under Rehum." Verse 22 speaks of "priests from the surrounding region." The priests might have excused themselves from heavy work, pleading that it was not their calling, but it is to their credit that they did not. Moreover, we read that when they had completed their assignments, they dedicated (or consecrated) both the Sheep Gate and the Tower of the Hundred to God, which shows how they regarded their labor. Their labor was unto God, and the product was for him.

Men of Jericho. Jericho was a good way off, and the men of Jericho might have argued that the reconstruction of Jerusalem was of little use to them. Later on, the residents of other cities are mentioned also: Tekoa, Gibeon,

Mizpah, Zanoah, Beth Hakkerem, Beth Zur, and Keilah. The same might have been said in their case. But they worked too.

Union Men or Guild Members. Verse 8 mentions "Uzziel son of Harhaiah, one of the goldsmiths" and "Hananiah, one of the perfume-makers." In verse 31 another goldsmith is mentioned, a man named Malkijah. More goldsmiths are mentioned in verse 32. These were skilled craftsmen who might have complained that the construction industry was not their field or even that the rough work of building might damage their delicate hands. But again, it appears they took on their fair share of the work.

City Officials. At several points in these lists are the names of people said to be rulers over certain districts or subdistricts: Rephaiah and Shallum, each "ruler of a half-district of Jerusalem"; Malkijah, "ruler of the district of Beth Hakkerem"; Shallum, "ruler of the district of Mizpah"; Nehemiah son of Azbuk, "ruler of a half-district of Beth Zur"; and Hashabiah and Binnui, each "ruler of a half-district of Keilah." It is important to note that these city officials or rulers were not above pitching in to work alongside the poor people of Jerusalem or the middle class.

Women. Women were not expected to do construction work, but some of them did, as verse 12 tells us. We are told of repairs made by Shallum, ruler of a half district of Jerusalem, "with the help of his daughters."

Bachelors. Cyril Barber notes astutely that certain bachelors also cooperated in the rebuilding of the wall although they obviously did not have either wives or children to protect. They are mentioned in verse 23. Their names were Benjamin and Hasshub, and they lived together in one house.

Temple Servants. These are mentioned in verse 26 as "living on the hill of Ophel" and as making repairs "up to a point opposite the Water Gate toward the east and the projecting tower." This was their area of the city, and they were taking responsibility for it. The temple servants are mentioned again toward the end (v. 31).

City Guards. One is mentioned, though there may have been others. His name was Shemaiah (v. 29). He would have been the Jews' equivalent of a security official or policeman.

Merchants. Finally, toward the end of the chapter, there is mention of merchants: "Between the room above the corner and the Sheep Gate the goldsmiths and merchants made repairs" (v. 32). It is natural to find the goldsmiths and merchants working together since they were of the same class and were in professions that would bring them together. What is surprising is finding the merchants working. Their business was trade. We might expect them to have been trading now, profiting by the situation. Apparently they were not. They were working with the others.

What a remarkable achievement! Yet in fairness (and perhaps as an encouragement to ourselves), it is necessary to say that Nehemiah did not achieve total success. The cooperation was remarkable, but according to verse 5, the nobles of Tekoa, unlike the other nobles, "would not put their shoulders to the work." Frank R. Tillapaugh, pastor of Bear Valley Church in Denver, Colorado, said of this verse in a public address, "There are always a few turkeys in the bunch." True enough! Nehemiah had them, and we will have our turkeys too.

It is worth noting, however, that the aloof disgruntlement of their leaders did not hinder the men of Tekoa. Not only did they build the section of the wall referred to in verse 5, but they apparently built another section too, after the first was finished. Nehemiah records this achievement in verse 27.

The success of Nehemiah in marshaling the entire population of Judah in this enterprise is something we need to take special note of, for today in the church everyone is also to be involved. Ephesians 4:11–13 tells us what the proper pattern is to be:

> It was he [Jesus] who gave some to be apostles, some to be prophets, some to be evangelists, and some to be pastors and teachers, to prepare God's people for works of service, so that the body of Christ may be built up until we all reach unity in the faith and in the knowledge of the Son of God and become mature, attaining to the whole measure of the fullness of Christ.

This is the basis of what Bible teachers today call "an every-member ministry." It means that the ministers in the churches are to prepare the people in the churches to do the churches' work. That is, clergy are to teach the laity, and the laity are to do the work of serving each other and the world.

Unfortunately, many churches have it completely turned around. It is said that today the churches resemble more than anything else a football game played in a large stadium. There are eighty thousand spectators in the stands who badly need some exercise, and there are twenty-two men on the field who badly need a rest.

A Coordinated Effort

Two more things need to be said about Nehemiah's relationship to his work. First, he coordinated the effort. He not only divided the task into manageable units and then assigned the right people to each part but also fit the whole together so there were no gaps and so each picked up where the other ones left off. We see this in such frequently repeated phrases as "the adjoining section," "the next section," and "next to them [him]."

Not only did Nehemiah coordinate the work so that no gaps were left and all worked closely to one another, but he also seems to have arranged the work in part for the convenience and motivation of the workers. Many were assigned to (or chose) portions of the wall in front of or directly adjacent to their houses—the priests rebuilding the area near the temple (vv. 1, 28), the temple servants the area near their dwelling on the temple mount (v. 26),

Jedaiah the portion of the wall "opposite his house" (v. 10), Benjamin and Hasshub the portion of the wall "in front of their house" (v. 23), and so on. This would be convenient for all, since no time would be lost in commuting back and forth or in going home for lunch. And it would ensure good work. A person would be certain to build strong walls where his own house needed to be protected.

The best management recognizes an element of self-interest in even the best workers and on even the most altruistic projects.

Recognition for Each Worker

The final element in Nehemiah's work relationship is that he seems to have recognized the accomplishments of each worker. The chapter itself suggests this, since it lists many. Still, without any doubt it is only a sample of what this great leader actually did. We can be sure that as he made the rounds of the builders, he called each by name and praised him or her for what he or she was achieving. Besides, Nehemiah would have written it down (there is a list of people who returned from the exile in chap. 7 and other important lists in chaps. 10–12). Somewhere there would have been a record of each one's contribution.

All but one! Have you noticed that in this long list of names Nehemiah's own name is not listed? He was as active as anyone, of course, even more so. We can be sure of that. But when it came to giving credit, he did not say, as Nebuchadnezzar, who had conquered Jerusalem more than 140 years earlier, said when looking out over his own city, "Is not this the great Babylon I have built as the royal residence, by my mighty power and for the glory of my majesty?" (Dan. 4:30). Nebuchadnezzar took glory for himself and was judged for it. By contrast, Nehemiah gave credit to others, listing what each had been assigned and what each had built. Then, when it was all over, he gave the ultimate glory to God, as he had done from the beginning. "This work had been done with the help of our God," was his conclusion (Neh. 6:16). We find here a pattern to emulate by those who desire to strive for excellence in leadership, the completion of worthy goals, and the glory of God.

5

The Fifth Dynamic:
Dealing with Opposition, Part 1

Nehemiah 4:1–23

When Sanballat heard that we were rebuilding the wall, he became angry and was greatly incensed. He ridiculed the Jews, and in the presence of his associates and the army of Samaria, he said, "What are those feeble Jews doing? Will they restore their wall? Will they offer sacrifices? Will they finish in a day? Can they bring the stones back to life from those heaps of rubble—burned as they are?"

Tobiah the Ammonite, who was at his side, said, "What they are building—if even a fox climbed up on it, he would break down their wall of stones!"

Hear us, O our God, for we are despised. Turn their insults back on their own heads. Give them over as plunder in a land of captivity. Do not cover up their guilt or blot out their sins from your sight, for they have thrown insults in the face of the builders.

So we rebuilt the wall till all of it reached half its height, for the people worked with all their heart.

But when Sanballat, Tobiah, the Arabs, the Ammonites and the men of Ashdod heard that the repairs to Jerusalem's walls had gone ahead and that the gaps were being closed, they were very angry. They all plotted together to come and fight against Jerusalem and stir up trouble against it. But we prayed to our God and posted a guard day and night to meet this threat.

Nehemiah 4:1–9

49

One day a farmer, who was a Quaker, was having trouble with his mule. He was trying to plow his field, and the mule was being unusually stubborn. He wouldn't move. So the Quaker decided to talk to him "reasonably." He said, "Thou knowest I am a Quaker. Thou knowest I can't curse thee. Thou knowest I can't whip thee. What thou does not know is that I can sell thee to my neighbor down the road. He is no Quaker, and he can beat the living daylights out of thee." We all have faced situations in which we feel like that Quaker. We are aware of ways we cannot or should not respond to opposition. What we want is a permissible way to whip it.

In the fourth, fifth, and sixth chapters of Nehemiah, we see how he dealt successfully with six forms of opposition.

Success Breeds Opposition

Opposition is almost always caused by success and not failure. The first thing we should know, if we are trying to do something worthwhile and are being opposed, is that it is because we are achieving something. We should be encouraged by it. We see this in Nehemiah's case in the very first verse of the chapter: "When Sanballat heard that we were rebuilding the wall, he became angry and was greatly incensed." The reason Sanballat was angry was that the wall was actually being rebuilt and he was threatened by Nehemiah's success. Nobody would have paid any attention if Nehemiah were failing.

Why do people oppose success? Why aren't they happy to see someone else succeed? Howard F. Vos suggests several reasons:

1. Some people are threatened by another person's success. As Vos says, "Some will oppose [another person or a work] because they stand to lose position or power or prestige politically, religiously, or socially."[1] Ours is a sinful world, and very few people are altruistic. They are out for themselves. Therefore, if one person moves forward, another sees it as diminishing his or her own prestige or position.

This was what was happening in the case of Nehemiah's opponents: Sanballat the Horonite, Tobiah the Ammonite, and the unnamed Arabs, Ammonites, and people of Ashdod associated with them. We have already been introduced to the two leaders in Nehemiah 2:10 and 19, where we are told that "they were very much disturbed that someone had come to promote the welfare of the Israelites" and that "they mocked and ridiculed us." Sanballat was called the Horonite because he came from the town of Beth Horon, about eight miles northwest of Jerusalem. He was now governor of the fortified city of Samaria to the north and no doubt wanted to have Jerusalem within his jurisdiction. Sanballat is mentioned in the Elephantine Papyri (discovered in Egypt, dating from 408–407 BC), where he is said to have been the governor of Samaria and to have had two sons.[2] Tobia was the governor of Ammon, which lay across the Jordan River to the east of Jerusalem.

In the old days, several great trade routes went through Jerusalem on the way to Egypt, Persia, Arabia, or Asia Minor. Sanballat and Tobiah perceived correctly that if Jerusalem were rebuilt, much of this valuable trade would return to it and their provinces would be diminished proportionately.

2. *Others are jealous.* Sometimes opposition arises not because there is any real threat to a person but because of simple jealousy. Sometimes a worker will criticize a colleague because the colleague is doing a better job or is working harder than he or she is. A woman will criticize another woman merely because she is more attractive, shows greater intelligence, or is more successful at her work. Jealousy is a cause of disharmony among leaders in the Christian church, though it is usually disguised as a doctrinal or ecclesiastical disagreement. One will attack another because "he is wrong in his eschatology" or because "he associated with liberals," but the real cause is jealousy of the other man's success.

This was a factor in the attacks of Sanballat and Tobiah on the Jews' project. They despised the Jews and were jealous of any attempts to improve their earthly prospects. That is why Nehemiah wrote in chapter 2, "They were very much disturbed that someone had come to promote the welfare of the Israelites" (v. 10).

3. *Some oppose others or their projects because they have a different agenda than they do.* Of all the reasons for opposition to a good work, this one is probably the most valid, though the reasons for preferring the objector's own project are not necessarily good. I place most of the opposition to Christian projects from today's secularists in this category. For example, when a liberal group sues a New England township to have a manger scene removed from the town square, where it has been for scores of Christmases, it is not because the manger is a threat to them or because of jealousy but because any display of religion is opposed to the secular agenda of this group. Such groups want to drive any visible signs of religion from life. In an increasingly secular culture such as we have in the United States today, we must expect opposition of this nature, and we must expect it to increase both in volume and intensity.

4. *Some feel excluded.* There may have been an element of exclusion in the opposition of Sanballat and Tobiah to the Jews' rebuilding project. They were not Jews, and the Jews were conscious of their unique ethnic origins and history. They did not want the assistance of their non-Jewish neighbors.

Sometimes this is right, and the resulting feelings of exclusion and opposition are inevitable. For example, the church has a unique identity and should preserve it. Membership in the visible body of Jesus Christ is for those who have trusted in Christ as their Savior from sin and who are attempting to follow him. The church is not a social club. If this by itself causes someone outside to feel excluded, and if he or she expresses this feeling of exclusion by opposing the church's program or projects, very little can be done to change the situation. On the other hand, many such feelings are unnecessary, and churches above all organizations should go out of their way to include all types of people. They should be among the most embracing rather than among the most exclusive institutions of society.

5. *People suspect the motivations of those they oppose.* This was one of the spoken reasons for Sanballat and Tobiah's opposition to Nehemiah, though it may have been only a cover-up for their less noble motivations. They accused the Jews of fortifying Jerusalem out of a desire to rebel against Persia: "What is this you are doing? . . . Are you rebelling against the king?" (Neh. 2:19). The Jews were not doing this, of course. Sanballat probably knew it. But it was a convenient and damaging charge to make. In a similar way, the stands Christians take for personal or social morality are often twisted by others to appear as mere bids for power or, worse yet, as plots to destroy civil liberties.

6. *Some people, especially leaders, lose face when others succeed.* This is something any successful person needs to be aware of and do everything possible to eliminate. The best way, whenever possible, is to take other people into the project and make them part of the success.

7. *Opposition comes from traditionalists—those who prefer the way things have been done in the past and do not want change.* This is common in the church where, for many people, religion has become a comfortable thing that promises much and asks little. In a church where nobody is expected to witness or serve or reach out to anybody, a program to transform that deadly attitude and unleash the church's potential will be rejected by most as undesirable.

8. *A final reason for opposition, at least to spiritual work, is that it is opposed by Satan.* Vos rightly cautions against attributing all opposition in either secular or Christian work to Satan:

> It would be easy to blame all of Nehemiah's difficulties on Satan's opposition, but that is too simplistic. . . . Satan merely needed to exploit already existing concerns. It is easy for the people of God to blame all their woes on Satan, as often it is easy for the western democracies to blame all their troubles on militant communism. But the truth is that Satan, like the communists, usually does not need to invent problems. He merely exploits or exacerbates existing conditions.[3]

That is true, of course. But it is also true that Satan is a powerful enemy and that he will do everything he can to destroy spiritual growth or Christian advance into territory he controls.

This is one reason Christian work in the inner city is so difficult. The cities are Satan's strongholds. Moreover, there are persons other than Satan who recognize God's work as God's work and oppose it because they hate God.

In light of these various reasons of opposition to a leader's success, it is obvious that any leader, whoever she or he is, will always be opposed by others and should be prepared for it. This is the fifth dynamic of leadership. The first involves the leader and God, the second the leader and his earthly superior or superiors, the third the leader and his subordinates, the fourth the leader and the task, the fifth the leader and his opposition. In pursuing this last point, we have seen eight reasons for opposition to a leader. We are now going to see the *forms* such opposition takes. In this and the next two chapters (chaps. 4–6), we will see how opposition came to Nehemiah and how he successfully contended with many different forms of opposition and overcame it.

Opposition by Ridicule

The easiest way to oppose something you do not like is to ridicule it, and this is the first thing Sanballat and Tobiah did. The text is vivid at this point, showing how Sanballat got Tobiah, his associates, and the army of Samaria together and made fun of the Jews in what must have been a great public forum: "What are those feeble Jews doing? Will they restore their wall? Will they offer sacrifices? Will they finish in a day? Can they bring the stones back to life from those heaps of rubble—burned as they are?" (v. 2).

Tobiah added, "What they are building—if even a fox climbed up on it, he would break down their wall of stones!" (v. 3).

The reason people ridicule those they oppose, aside from it being so easy, is that it is demoralizing and frequently effective. It is effective because it strikes at the hidden insecurity or weakness that almost everybody has. This is what was going on. Each of Sanballat's five rhetorical questions and Tobiah's taunt struck at a legitimate sense of weakness that Nehemiah and the others must have had.

"What are those feeble Jews doing?" This was directly to the point. The Jews were feeble, and they knew it. How could anyone as weak as they were hope to rebuild their city's walls?

"Will they restore their wall?" Indeed! How could they restore a wall one and one-half to two and one-half miles in circumference? It had been built by people more numerous and stronger than they were. How could they even hope to reassemble those huge stones?

"Will they offer sacrifices?" Most commentators take this question as referring to sacrifices of thanksgiving to be offered after the walls were finished. But I think Derek Kidner is correct when he regards it as probably meaning, "Are those fanatics going to *pray* the wall up? It's their only hope!"[4] The taunt was an attack on the Jews' faith, which was not that strong anyway, as we are going to see. Don't you find it difficult when someone ridicules your faith? "Maybe you think God's going to help you!" or "Why don't you go home and pray about it [chuckle]?" they say. It is difficult not to be unsettled by such ridicule.

"Will they finish in a day?" This means, "Don't they realize what an enormous task they are taking on?" This was effective because the Jews knew exactly how huge the task was.

"Can they bring the stones back to life from those heaps of rubble—burned as they are?" This was an exaggeration. The gates had been burned but not the walls. They were not limestone, which might well have been calcined by the intense heat of the fire that had been used to destroy Jerusalem at the time of Nebuchadnezzar's conquest. The walls were not crumbled, only tumbled. But the question was nevertheless effective in reminding the Jews of the great and overwhelming dimensions of the task.

Tobiah's taunt, "What they are building—if even a fox climbed up on it, he would break down their wall of stones!" had bite because, as excavation of these walls has shown, they did not turn out to be of the same quality as those that stood before them.

These were all very effective points, as I have indicated. Yet the point cannot be missed that the only reason they were being uttered was that something important was nevertheless going forward and was perceived by these two governors as being likely to succeed. Their anger revealed their fear that what they were ridiculing might actually come to pass.

How did Nehemiah deal with this attack? We need to see three things: one he did not do, and two he did.

First, he did not retaliate. The first thing most of us do when we are ridiculed is snap back. We would say, "So they think we're feeble, do they? Well, they're not so strong themselves. Sanballat, you're just a petty governor of a petty province of a remote area of the empire. Tobiah, you're only governor of that hot little desert area of Ammon. Who would want to live there?" Nehemiah did not do that. If he had, he would merely have lowered himself to the level of his critics, and he would have come out second best since they were stronger and more important than he was in the eyes of the world.

Second, Nehemiah prayed. This is important not only because it means he turned to God for help, as he always did, but also because he did not merely bottle up his feelings or try to suppress them, which would have solved nothing. Rather, he poured out his soul before the Lord. He admitted that he was hurt and angry: "We are despised" (v. 4). Nevertheless, the work was God's, and Nehemiah was therefore able to put it into God's hands and let him be the arbiter of the dispute and the judge of the Jews' opponents. "Turn their insults back on their own heads," Nehemiah said. "Give them over as plunder in a land of captivity. Do not cover up their guilt or blot out their sins from your sight, for they have thrown insults in the face of the builders" (vv. 4–5).[5]

What was the result of Nehemiah's prayer? He does not tell us explicitly. But the first great benefit was undoubtedly that it diffused his anger, since he does not show anger as he proceeds. This was valuable because anger is seldom productive and is usually a hindrance to good work. In addition, the prayer must have restored Nehemiah's perspective, if he was wavering. Instead of being thrown off by his enemies' ridicule, he now recognized it for what it was—fear that under his leadership the Jews might actually succeed—and he understood that the best thing the Jews could do was press on with their task.

Third, Nehemiah went on with the work. Since he had left the taunts of his enemies with God, he no longer needed to be concerned about them and could get on with the task God had given him. What he says is nice: "So we rebuilt the wall till all of it reached half its height, for the people worked with all their heart" (v. 6).

It was the ancient version of the World War II slogan: "Praise the Lord and pass the ammunition!"

Opposition by the Threat of Violence

The larger second half of Nehemiah 4 contains a second form of opposition to the governor's work: the threat of physical violence. Nehemiah introduces the problem in verses 7 and 8 and describes how he met it in verses 9–23. The introductory verses say, "But when Sanballat, Tobiah, the Arabs, the Ammonites, and the men of Ashdod heard that the repairs to Jerusalem's walls had gone ahead and that the gaps were being closed, they were very angry. They all plotted together to come and fight against Jerusalem and stir up trouble against it."

Three things need to be seen to appreciate the force of this second form of opposition.

1. It came at a low point in the people's circumstances, when they were tired. The people had been working with all their heart, as Nehemiah records (v. 6). The wall had reached half its height. But there was still half of the wall to go, and the strength and resolve of the people were already beginning to give out. We see this in the report of the people of Judah, recorded in verse 10: "The strength of the laborers is giving out, and there is so much rubble that we cannot rebuild the wall."

Haven't you felt that kind of discouragement yourself when you were in the middle of a particularly demanding job? I have. I often feel it when I am in the middle of writing a sermon. In fact, I have a term for it. I say to myself that I have "bogged," meaning that I have bogged down. It is because the process of preparing a sermon is mentally and emotionally draining, and I frequently reach a point at which I no longer want to go on. If when I am feeling like that I should receive an additional threat from outside, the combination of tiredness and fear or anxiety could easily make me stop what I am doing. We can fight against one enemy on one front, but it is hard to fight against two (or more) enemies simultaneously.

2. It came from powerful foes. Up to this point, we have only been told about Sanballat the governor of Samaria and Tobiah the governor of Ammon, though a third man, Geshem the Arab, was mentioned in 2:19. Now suddenly there are four distinct groups: (1) Sanballat of Samaria, (2) Tobiah of Ammon and his people, (3) the Arabs, and (4) the men of Ashdod. In other words, the opposition was not going away just because Nehemiah had prayed about it. On the contrary, it was increasing and it was threatening. To realize the full force of this threat, we need to visualize it geographically. Samaria was to the north. Ammon was to the east. The Arabs were to the south. The people of Ashdod (or Philistia) were to the west. In other words, the opposition of Sanballat and Tobiah was now a coalition of those who together entirely surrounded Jerusalem.

Moreover, they were doing two things: (1) they were plotting (v. 8), and (2) they were threatening the Jews (v. 11). "Before they know it or see us, we will be right there among them and will kill them and put an end to the work."

3. It was effective. It is not surprising in light of the first two points that this form of opposition was effective, at least upon the people who lived near these enemies but who were helping to rebuild Jerusalem. They knew the strength of these foes and reported, apparently with genuine fear and discouragement, "Wherever you turn, they will attack us" (v. 12).

It was a critical point in the project, and the people probably would have abandoned the work were it not for Nehemiah. He had been praying. Prayer had provided him with balance. He knew the strength of this threat, but he also knew its limitations. Above all, he knew the strength of God, who he was sure was on his side.

In military terms, Nehemiah must have known it was unlikely that his enemies would attack the city in full force, since he had the imposing authority of Artaxerxes behind him. If the coalition of the governors of Trans-Euphrates attacked him, they would be opposing Artaxerxes, the very thing they were accusing the Jews of doing. On the other hand, Nehemiah must have known that what we might call guerrilla warfare was likely. It would not take much of an effort for his enemies to sneak up on the city, surprise the builders, and kill some—and deny that they had anything to do with it. Besides, he knew that anything of this nature would so demoralize the people that the work would stop and would never get going again. What was Nehemiah to do? What he did was extremely wise. He dealt with the real threat, not the imagined one, and did so in a way that built the people's low self-esteem and strengthened their resolve.

Nehemiah turned Jerusalem into an armed camp.

When the threat became known, he responded by posting a guard day and night (v. 9). When the rumors of violence continued and began to have a demoralizing effect, he went further: (1) he stopped the work (cf. vv. 13, 15),

(2) he armed the people (v. 13), and (3) he arranged the people in family groups at the most exposed places along the wall (v. 13). Dividing them into families corresponded with Israel's traditional way of fighting and heightened each person's awareness of the stakes. Nehemiah knew they would fight most fiercely when the lives of their own families were in jeopardy.

When his enemies learned of the Jews' preparation and that their plot was frustrated, the pressure lessened and Nehemiah was able to return the workers to the walls. But he did not forget the threat. Therefore, (1) he divided the people into two groups, one that would work and one that would be in readiness to fight at any time (even the workers carried arms, vv. 16–18); (2) he devised a plan for meeting an unexpected attack (vv. 18–20); (3) he accelerated the pace of the building (from dawn until the stars came out, v. 21); and (4) he kept the people in the city day and night (v. 23). Most important, throughout this period he continued to boost morale by reminding everyone that God would fight for them: "Don't be afraid of them. Remember the Lord, who is great and awesome, and fight for your brothers, your sons and your daughters, your wives and your homes" (v. 14), and "Our God will fight for us!" (v. 20).

Nehemiah also stood with the people through it all. "Neither I nor my brothers nor my men nor the guards with me took off our clothes; each had his weapon, even when he went for water" (v. 23).

What a pattern for us when we are faced with opposition: prayer and persistence, faith and good works.

But faith most of all. Nehemiah had many good traits, and he was a leader even by worldly standards. But what made him really great was his faith in God and his assurance that the God who had given him the task of rebuilding the wall would stand by him until the job was done. The apostle Paul wrote that God keeps at *his* work until the job is done: "Being confident of this, that he who began a good work in you will carry it on to completion until the day of Christ Jesus" (Phil. 1:6). We should know that he will enable us to carry our work to its completion too.

6

The Fifth Dynamic:
Dealing with Opposition, Part 2

Nehemiah 5:1–19

Now the men and their wives raised a great outcry against their Jewish brothers. Some were saying, "We and our sons and daughters are numerous; in order for us to eat and stay alive, we must get grain."

Others were saying, "We are mortgaging our fields, our vineyards and our homes to get grain during the famine."

Still others were saying, "We have had to borrow money to pay the king's tax on our fields and vineyards. Although we are of the same flesh and blood as our countrymen and though our sons are as good as theirs, yet we have to subject our sons and daughters to slavery. Some of our daughters have already been enslaved, but we are powerless, because our fields and our vineyards belong to others."

When I heard their outcry and these charges, I was very angry. I pondered them in my mind and then accused the nobles and officials. I told them, "You are exacting usury from your own countrymen!" So I called together a large meeting to deal with them and said: "As far as possible, we have bought back our Jewish brothers who were sold to the Gentiles. Now you are selling your brothers, only for them to be sold back to us!" They kept quiet, because they could find nothing to say.

So I continued, "What you are doing is not right. Shouldn't you walk in the fear of our God to avoid the reproach of our Gentile enemies? I and my brothers and my men are also lending the people money and grain. But let the exacting of usury stop! Give back to

them immediately their fields, vineyards, olive groves and houses, and also the usury you
are charging them—the hundredth part of the money, grain, new wine and oil."

"We will give it back," they said. "And we will not demand anything more from them.
We will do as you say."

Nehemiah 5:1–12

The distribution of material in Nehemiah 1–6 is interesting. One chapter is given to Nehemiah's reaction to the challenge to build Jerusalem's walls; one chapter to his audience with Artaxerxes, his trip to Jerusalem, and his nighttime inspection of the ruins; a third chapter to the way the walls were built. But then three whole chapters (chaps. 4–6) discuss the opposition Nehemiah encountered while building the wall and how he dealt with it.

The distribution shows how important a leader's approach to opposition is. To succeed at a task when there is no opposition requires skill, but it takes the skill of a leader to succeed when the work is being opposed. John White strikes this note in reference to Christian leaders in his study of *Excellence in Leadership*:

> No test of leadership is more revealing than the test of opposition. Christian leaders can go to pieces under such pressure. Some grow too discouraged to continue. Others build walls around themselves and shoot murderously from behind them. They become embattled, embittered and vindictive. Not so Nehemiah. Nowhere does his leadership shine more brilliantly than in his handling of opposition.[1]

In chapter 4 we saw how Nehemiah faced two common forms of opposition: ridicule, the easiest of all forms of opposition, and the threat of violence. The latter is the path often taken when ridicule fails. Nehemiah overcame the first by recognizing ridicule for what it was: a weak attempt to get him to stop the building. He followed up in two ways: he took the matter to God in prayer, looking to him for vindication, and he kept building. Nehemiah overcame the second attack by such practical means as arming his workers, posting guards, keeping the people in the city at night where they would be safe, and establishing procedures for unexpected attacks. These devices were successful. His enemies were frustrated, and the work advanced relentlessly.

Suddenly, to judge from the tone of chapter 5, a new form of opposition erupted and from an unexpected source. The first two forms of opposition had been from without, from Israel's enemies. This new form was from within. It arose because of wrong conduct by some of the Jewish people themselves.

Isn't that the way it always is? You are engaged in some important work. You have been opposed by people who are not Christians and do not share the vision. You have overcome that form of opposition and are pressing on, when suddenly there is a problem within the church or Christian community itself. Often this threat is more of a problem than the external threat. It had been true of Israel before this. During the days of the monarchy, the Jewish states had been opposed by their pagan neighbors. There had been many wars. But when God sent prophets to recall the people to righteousness, it was not the pagans who killed God's messengers but the Jews themselves. In the same way, an examination of church history will show that the most successful attacks upon the church have come not from unbelievers but from those within, from people who have professed to know God and Jesus Christ. They have been from "Christians" promoting heresy or "believers" denouncing, persecuting, or even killing other Christians.

Who is responsible for most opposition to Christian work today? Is it the government with its radical "separation of church and state" policies? Is it the American Civil Liberties Union with its strong bias against religion? These can be sources of genuine opposition, and they are. But is it not true that the greatest opposition to Christian work today is from those within the church who want a form of godliness but who reject genuine Christianity?

The cartoon character Pogo said, "We have met the enemy and he is us." Nehemiah found this to be the case in his day, and we will too.

Exploiting the Poor

The problem that erupted internally at this point is described very well in verses 1–5:

> Now the men and their wives raised a great outcry against their Jewish brothers. Some were saying, "We and our sons and daughters are numerous; in order for us to eat and stay alive, we must get grain."
>
> Others were saying, "We are mortgaging our fields, our vineyards and our homes to get grain during the famine."
>
> Still others were saying, "We have had to borrow money to pay the king's tax on our fields and vineyards. Although we are of the same flesh and blood as our countrymen and though our sons are as good as theirs, yet we have to subject our sons and daughters to slavery. Some of our daughters have already been enslaved, but we are powerless, because our fields and our vineyards belong to others."

These verses describe a classic example of the gap between rich and poor and the way the rich sometimes tend to control things so that they get richer while the poor get poorer. It was a case of pure exploitation, and what made it worse was that it occurred within the Jewish community among those who should have been helping one another.

Originally the Jews who had returned to Israel from Babylon were well-off. Cyril Barber reminds us that, according to the first chapters of Ezra, those who had come back from the exile returned with many worldly goods. Ezra gave an inventory of their possessions, reporting in summary that there were fifty-four hundred articles of gold and silver (Ezra 1:11). In addition, King Cyrus had himself opened his treasury and had contributed "the articles belonging to the temple of the LORD, which Nebuchadnezzar had carried away from Jerusalem" (Ezra 1:7; cf. 2 Chron. 36:18; Dan. 1:1–2). Once in Jerusalem, many of the Jews were either wealthy enough or had prospered sufficiently to panel their homes, a luxury at one time reserved only for kings (Hag.1:4). When the temple was built, the people gave generously for its embellishment (Neh. 7:71–72).

Besides, only thirteen years before Nehemiah's arrival, a second group of exiles had returned with Ezra, and these had brought additional "silver and gold" and "the freewill offerings of the people" left in Babylon (Ezra 7:16). Other gifts from Babylon seem to have been arriving regularly (Zech. 6:10).[2]

What changed this advantageous situation? Why, by the time we reach Nehemiah 5, are some of the people so poor?

There were several factors. One of the cries of the people recorded in chapter 5 mentions famine. A lack of rain and the consequent failure of the crops was one problem. Others complained about the king's taxation, though scholars generally agree that this was not particularly burdensome, at least not for any but the extremely poor. These were contributing factors, but the real problem—which Nehemiah seemed to get to immediately—is that the wealthier Jews had been exploiting those who were less well-off and actually reducing some of them to the desperate state of slavery. Exploiting? Perhaps that is too strong a word. The wealthy would never have used it. They would have claimed that they were merely lending money in perfectly legal ways, perhaps even doing it to "help" their poorer countrymen. But whether it was technically legal or not, the rich were certainly taking advantage of the situation. As Nehemiah says later, their actions were "not right" (v. 9).

Barber suggests that there were three classes of people being exploited: (1) workers whose resources had been used up (v. 2), (2) farmers whose lands were being mortgaged (v. 3), and (3) people having trouble paying taxes (vv. 4–5). If this was so, those in the third category were the worst off because they had already lost their fields and were in the process of losing some of their sons and daughters through slavery.

But the situation was probably not as clear-cut as that. Most of those in category one would have been farmers also, so all three were tillers of the land. All were affected by the famine and by the exploitation. Probably the complaints in verses 1–5 are expressions of an increasingly desperate situation to which any one of the poor could be subject. The sequence would be: (1) a lack of adequate food, or hunger, (2) the mortgaging of the fields for short-term cash to buy grain and pay taxes, (3) loss of the fields because of an inability to repay what was borrowed, and (4) the selling of sons and daughters either into indentured service or outright slavery for the sake of survival. The details are different, but there is a similarly downward-spiraling sequence among the poor today. And like today, it was the poor, not the well-off, who protested the injustice.

A Time for Anger

How is a leader to deal with injustices, particularly when they are practiced by the influential against the uninfluential? How can a person confront evil when the strong have the law on their side? The first thing Nehemiah tells us is that he got angry about these injustices: "When I heard their outcry and these charges, I was very angry" (v. 6).

As I have read the various commentaries on Nehemiah, I have been amused to see how much contemporary writers struggle over Nehemiah's anger. This is because anger seems basically wrong to them. John White wrestles with whether Nehemiah's anger was just or merely carnal, and with whether, assuming it was at least largely carnal, it was better to express or repress it.[3]

Cyril Barber recognizes the difference between righteous and unrighteous anger and finds Nehemiah's response to be that of a godly man. But he regards anger as so much of a problem that he interrupts his exposition with a section on "how to handle it."[4] In fact, it is not only commentators who have struggled with Nehemiah's anger. Translators have done it too. For example, at verse 7 the New English Bible reads, "I mastered my feelings and reasoned with the nobles," implying that the anger of verse 6 was wrong. The New International Version is surely closer to the truth when it says, "I pondered them [the charges] in my mind and then accused the nobles." The Revised Standard Version states forcefully, "I took counsel with myself, and I brought charges."

There is a great difference between righteous and unrighteous anger, and we are frequently angry only in the second sense, when something is offensive to us personally. But while we need to be warned against such anger, we also need urging to be angry when righteous anger is appropriate.

Some years ago Franky Schaeffer, son of the late evangelical author and Christian apologist Francis A. Schaeffer, wrote a book entitled *A Time for Anger: The Myth of Neutrality*. It began, "There are times in which anyone with a shred of moral principle should be profoundly angry. We live in such times."[5]

In my view the book is not a particularly good one because it lashes out only against the secular culture and not against the injustices perpetrated by the Christian community. After all, what are we to expect from the world but injustice? Even Nehemiah was not angry at Sanballat and Tobiah. He simply realized where they were coming from and made whatever arrangements were necessary to oppose them. Real anger should be felt for those who profess to walk by God's standards and yet compromise those high standards by their actions. Nevertheless, I like the title of Schaeffer's book, because it says rightly that there is "a time for anger" and alerts us to it. Nehemiah was angry. The exploitation of Jews by Jews was not right, and he was angry enough to oppose it.

Rebuking Offenders

As Nehemiah "pondered" this problem rather than acting precipitously, he chose a response path in which he confronted the offenders privately. He reports this briefly: "I told them, 'You are exacting usury from your own countrymen'" (v. 7). We can assume that in doing this Nehemiah amplified his charge by showing that what they were doing was against the Old Testament. He would have pointed to passages such as Exodus 22:25: "If you lend money to one of my people among you who is needy, do not be like a moneylender; charge him no interest." Or the great "Jubilee chapter" of Leviticus:

> If one of your countrymen becomes poor and is unable to support himself among you, help him as you would an alien or a temporary resident, so he can continue to live among you. Do not take interest of any kind from him, but fear your God, so that your countryman may continue to live among you. You must not lend him money at interest or sell him food at a profit. . . . If one of your countrymen becomes poor among you and sells himself to you, do not make him work as a slave. He is to be treated as a hired worker or a temporary resident among you; he is to work for you until the Year of Jubilee. Then he and his children are to be released, and he will go back to his own clan and to the property of his forefathers.
>
> Leviticus 25:35–37, 39–41

Or Deuteronomy 23:19: "Do not charge your brother interest, whether on money or food or anything else that may earn interest."

According to these verses, Jews were not to exploit their countrymen. They could lend money to outsiders at going rates, but Jews were their own people and they were not to take advantage of them in any way. Moreover, if a Jew fell into slavery, free Jews were to do everything possible to redeem him and have him set free. Nehemiah refers to this obligation later.

What Nehemiah was doing in this private confrontation with the wealthy was following the first (and possibly the second) principle for dealing with sin among brothers, which Jesus spelled out in Matthew 18: "If your brother sins against you, go and show him his fault, just between the two of you. If he listens to you, you have won your brother over. But if he will not listen, take one or two others along, so that 'every matter may be established by the testimony of two or three witnesses'" (vv. 15–16). We do not know whether Nehemiah had witnesses along for the first one-on-one meeting with the offending nobles and officials, but he was following the general procedure. Before he made things public, Nehemiah was trying to resolve the problem privately.

Did he succeed? Apparently not. There was no response from the nobles. They seem merely to have dug in their heels and said nothing, as people in the wrong often do. Nehemiah moved to a public confrontation.

The Public Confrontation

At this point, I am indebted to Frank R. Tillapaugh for some important thoughts, based on the fact that in order to have a public meeting Nehemiah must have pulled his workers off the wall. In normal circumstances this would not have been remarkable, but these were not normal circumstances. Nehemiah's one goal was to build the wall and to build it quickly before the effort could be stopped by Israel's enemies. He had everyone working. They were working from the dawn's first light until the stars came out. In fact, from the moment three days after he had arrived in Jerusalem, when he had begun the building, until now, there had been only one small interval in which the work had been stopped, and that was when a hostile armed attack had seemed imminent (Neh. 4:13–14). As soon as the threat passed, Nehemiah had the people back on the walls again.

Yet now Nehemiah stopped the work and held a public meeting. Why was this? Tillapaugh says it was because the situation had changed. There was a problem within now, and it was of such overriding importance that it was necessary to deal with it immediately. "What good was it to build the wall," asked Tillapaugh, "if inside the wall there were people who were exploiting one another?"[6]

We must ask that question again today, and we must ask it of ourselves. What good is it to build great evangelical institutions, constructing walls against the "evil" of our opposing, secular world, if within the walls the so-called people of God are indistinguishable from those without? What good is it to preserve a separate "Christian" identity if Christians behave like unbelievers? To put it in sharp terms, we need to stop calling the world to repent until we repent ourselves.

Of what should we repent? There are scores of things, but a thoughtful consideration of this chapter suggests two of them.

1. Disobedience to the revealed law of God. The nobles of Nehemiah's day were disobeying the teachings of Exodus, Leviticus, and Deuteronomy. Why is it that so many within the evangelical church take the revealed law of God so casually? It is no surprise that the world does this. The world does not receive the Bible as God's Book. But we do. We even maintain that it is inerrant "in the whole and in its parts." How then can we take it so lightly? How can we say, as I have heard many so-called evangelicals say, "But that [specific teaching] was for that day, not today." Or, "Well, we have to be realistic. Life just doesn't fit those clear-cut categories." We play loose with the Scriptures, and we need to repent of it. We need to become people of the Book—in fact, and not just in our profession.

2. *Putting our personal prosperity before other people's well-being.* That is what these nobles were doing. They were enriching themselves at the expense of poor people. May I suggest that the evangelical church has been doing that too—or at least enriching itself while disregarding its poorer members. The only times in history in which the church has been really godly and really strong have been times when it was out rubbing shoulders with the poor and helping them. Revival has always borne fruit among the masses. John Wesley and George Whitefield preached in the fields to common people, not in cathedrals to the privileged. But most of us do not even know the poor. We will give contributions to help them, sometimes—if we are not asked for too much. But we are not a church of the poor. We are not even a church of the masses. We need to repent of our elitist dispositions.

What is our problem? Isn't it our love of money, the very thing that was causing the officials of Nehemiah's day to exploit those around them? Don't we put the good life for ourselves first, at whatever cost?

I cannot say that the evangelical church is consciously exploiting other Christians or even the poor generally, though we are part of a system that makes it difficult for the poor to survive. But listen to this: "We and our sons and daughters are numerous; in order for us to eat and stay alive, we must get grain. . . . We are mortgaging our . . . homes to get grain. . . . We have had to borrow money . . . we are powerless" (vv. 2–5). It is all very timely and relevant because, whether or not we exploit them, we certainly do very little to help out the poor.

Frank Tillapaugh speaks of a city in which a suburban white Christian school got into financial trouble and the evangelical community immediately aroused itself to help out. But in the same city the struggles of an inner-city school were ignored.

Young Life thrives in the suburbs. In poor areas, Young Life can barely find money to pay a skeleton crew, yet the problems of the cities are greater than those in the outlying white areas.

We raise money to feed the poor in Bangladesh, so long as the campaigns do not cramp our own materialistic pursuits. But we do nothing to feed the poor on our doorsteps. We need to repent of such wickedness. We need to get right within the walls before we build the walls higher.

Nehemiah Succeeded

The astonishing thing about this chapter is that Nehemiah succeeded. We know that he faced stiff opposition, because the nobles did not respond when he approached them earlier. Nevertheless, after Nehemiah had exposed the wrong being done and had challenged the offenders to return the pledged fields, vineyards, olive groves, and houses, refund the interest, and stop the usury, the nobles responded, "We will give it back . . . we will not demand anything more from them. We will do as you say" (v. 12).

Nehemiah made sure it happened. He called the priests and had the nobles and officials take an oath to do what they had promised. It was the equivalent of drafting a notarized agreement. Then he performed a symbolic act, shaking out his garments as a prophetic warning that God would "shake down" anyone who had promised to do the right thing but then later reneged on it. John White makes a point of Nehemiah's action:

> Nehemiah's actions up to that point could have been taken nowadays by any upright humanist. Calling on priests to administer an oath can represent a legality having only a form of godliness. Every day godless witnesses swear over Bibles in human courts. But to exact prophetic judgment marked Nehemiah as a man who really did believe in the powers of the world to come and who was in touch with God—not only a transcendent God, but one who was immanent and close to his servants.[7]

That was Nehemiah's secret, after all. He was close to God. He had his priorities right and set a consistent example. In fact, in verses 14–18 Nehemiah reveals what his example was. He did not take the perquisites that might rightly have come to him because of his office: taxes and the good life. On the contrary, he lived out of his own means and used his personal abundance to feed those who were less fortunate. Those who were associated with him followed the pattern. They gave and worked too. It was a magnificent example of servant leadership, and it was because Nehemiah feared God. "Out of reverence for God I did not act like that," he said, contrasting his actions to those of worldly governors (v. 15).

That is our pattern. It is the pattern of Jesus who "did not come to be served, but to serve, and to give his life as a ransom for many" (Matt. 20:28). If we lead that way, we will be able to say, as Nehemiah does in closing, "Remember me with favor, O my God, for all I have done for these people" (v. 19).

7

The Fifth Dynamic:
Dealing with Opposition, Part 3

Nehemiah 6:1-14

When word came to Sanballat, Tobiah, Geshem the Arab and the rest of our enemies that I had rebuilt the wall and not a gap was left in it—though up to that time I had not set the doors in the gates—Sanballat and Geshem sent me this message: "Come, let us meet together in one of the villages on the plain of Ono."

But they were scheming to harm me; so I sent messengers to them with this reply: "I am carrying on a great project and cannot go down. Why should the work stop while I leave it and go down to you?" Four times they sent me the same message, and each time I gave them the same answer.

Then, the fifth time, Sanballat sent his aide to me with the same message, and in his hand was an unsealed letter in which was written:

"It is reported among the nations—and Geshem says it is true—that you and the Jews are plotting to revolt, and therefore you are building the wall. Moreover, according to these reports you are about to become their king and have even appointed prophets to make this proclamation about you in Jerusalem: 'There is a king in Judah!' Now this report will get back to the king: so come, let us confer together."

I sent him this reply: "Nothing like what you are saying is happening: you are just making it up out of your head."

. . . One day I went to the house of Shemaiah son of Delaiah, the son of Mehetabel, who was shut in at his home. He said, "Let us meet in the house of God, inside the

temple, and let us close the temple doors, because men are coming to kill you—by night they are coming to kill you."

But I said, "Should a man like me run away? Or should one like me go into the temple to save his life? I will not go!" I realized that God had not sent him, but that he had prophesied against me because Tobiah and Sanballat had hired him. He had been hired to intimidate me so that I would commit a sin by doing this, and then they would give me a bad name to discredit me.

Nehemiah 6:1–8, 10–13

In the last two chapters of Nehemiah, we have seen three forms of opposition, each of which threatened to defeat Nehemiah's plan to rebuild the wall of Jerusalem. The first two were external and came from Nehemiah's pagan enemies: (1) opposition by ridicule and (2) opposition by the threat of violence. Nehemiah overcame these by faith in God, courage, and practical wisdom. The third form of opposition was internal. It was caused by greed, which resulted in oppression of the poor by Israel's wealthy classes. Nehemiah overcame this problem by a procedure similar to the one outlined by Jesus in Matthew 18:15–17. He confronted the wrongdoers, first privately and then publicly, when they refused to listen.

With the internal dissension behind him, Nehemiah once again returned the workers to the wall and soon made such progress that within a short time the entire wall was completed to its full height. Only the gates remained to be constructed.

Suddenly, just when the work seemed about to be finished, a final phase of his enemies' opposition unfolded. It was in three parts: (1) opposition by intrigue, (2) opposition by innuendo, and (3) opposition by intimidation. Each was subtle; on the surface it appeared to be something other than what it was. Part of the challenge for Nehemiah was to see the real situation clearly.

Another characteristic was that each attack was aimed at Nehemiah personally. This had not been true before. The first two hindrances were to ridicule the Jews for their weaknesses and then to threaten them with violence, trying to make them afraid. The internal problems were between the poor and the rich who were exploiting them. Not so now. In the final phase of Sanballat and Tobiah's opposition, the attacks were aimed at Nehemiah. Cyril Barber says, "When Sanballat had his co-conspirators realize that they have been outmaneuvered, outgeneraled, and outwitted by Nehemiah, they decide to attack him personally. . . . Their wounded pride will not be appeased until Nehemiah has been humiliated."[1]

It was an old ploy. "Sack the quarterback," a coach will tell his defensive line. "Shoot at the officers," a commander will sometimes tell his troops.

At first this kind of opposition seems unwise and potentially useless, since to attack the leader is to attack the strongest rather than the weakest point of the opposing line. It is the reason opposition usually does not start at this point but rather with such easy things as ridicule and threats. Later on in the battle, it is different. Leaders get tired too, and the stress of leading a great project takes its toll. At this point, an attack on the leader is frequently effective.

Yet such attacks were not effective with Nehemiah. He held his ground. In noticing how he did it, we uncover further qualities of leadership in this extraordinary man.

Opposition by Intrigue

I just said that each of these final forms of opposition was characterized by its subtlety, that is, by appearing to be something other than what it was. This was particularly true of the approach recounted in verses 1–4: "When word came to Sanballat, Tobiah, Geshem the Arab and the rest of our enemies that I had rebuilt the wall and not a gap was left in it—though up to that time I had not set the doors in the gates—Sanballat and Geshem sent me this message: 'Come, let us meet together in one of the villages on the plain of Ono'" (vv. 1–2).

The reason this communication was subtle and therefore dangerous was that on the surface it sounded quite plausible. What is more, it was attractive. If the invitation for a conference had come earlier, surely Nehemiah would have been suspicious. It would have been an obvious ploy to get him to stop working. But now the wall was rebuilt; only the gates remained to be set in place. The project was finished—almost.

At such a time, the invitation seemed to be a concession speech by a person who had just lost a political campaign. "Nehemiah, it is no use pretending that we have not been opposed to your project. We have been. It has not been in our best interests. We have had our differences over it. But you have succeeded in spite of us, and now there is no use to carry on our opposition. For better or worse, we are going to have to live together, you as governor of Jerusalem and ourselves as governors of our own provinces. So let's be friends. What we need is a summit conference. Why don't we meet on the plain of Ono? It is a neutral site about equidistant from each of our provinces. You pick a village in Ono, and we'll meet you there." Since Nehemiah was already looking past the completion of the wall to further reforms, as the remainder of the book shows, an approach like this must have seemed both reasonable and attractive.

What was wrong with holding such a conference?

Isn't dialogue good? Isn't it always better to talk than to fight, to keep the lines of communication open?

Isn't a refusal to talk to our opponents always unnecessarily and unreasonably belligerent?

Isn't there a time to let bygones be bygones, to bury the hatchet?

What possible reason can there be for refusing to talk once the election is over or the job is done?

That was just the problem: the job was not done. True, it was *almost* done. The walls were completed to their full height. Only the gates remained. *But the gates remained,* and until they were completed, the entire great project was in jeopardy. Nehemiah knew this, and for that reason—at least this was one reason—he declined the invitation. What magnificent, single-minded concentration! And what a classic reply! "I am carrying on a great project and cannot go down. Why should the work stop while I leave it and go down to you?" (v. 3). Nehemiah reports that Sanballat and Geshem sent him the same message four times and that each time he gave them the same answer.

There are two characteristics of leadership that are particularly noticeable in this reply.

First, a leader must know how to say no. Some people can't seem to do that. Whether because of their own insecurity, an unbalanced desire always to please other people, or something else, they break down and give in—particularly if the request is repeated. Nehemiah said no four times.

"Shouldn't I be available for others?" someone asks.

Yes, of course. But there is a difference between living as a servant of God and living to win the approval of man.

In what circumstances should I say no? When I am faced by temptation. When I am being asked to compromise the truth or morality. When a lesser good threatens to undermine a higher one.

To whom should I way no? To my children, quite often. To enemies. To friends who would distract me from God's call. To Satan.

When should I say no? Whenever necessary, and far more often than I do.

The second quality of leadership noticeable in Nehemiah's reply to Sanballat and Geshem was his practical wisdom. We see it in how he receives the message and in how he replies to it. He was not taken in. Although the communication sounded plausible, Nehemiah knew that the governors were actually scheming to harm him. He says so in verse 2. Again, although he knew their intent, Nehemiah did not unnecessarily antagonize them. He did not denounce them for their perfidy. He merely said that he was too busy to go down to the plain of Ono. It would have taken him at least a day to get there, a day for the conference, and another day to get back. He was unwilling to spare those three days.

Cyril Barber says, "His ability to see the issues clearly and stand firm under pressure safeguarded him from succumbing to the wiles of his adversaries."[2]

Opposition by Innuendo

After the fourth communication to Nehemiah and his fourth refusal (v. 4), Sanballat must have sensed that his anxiety was showing and something else was required. So he resorted to innuendo. Here is how Nehemiah tells it in verses 5–7:

> Then, the fifth time, Sanballat sent his aide to me with the same message, and in his hand was an unsealed letter in which was written:

> "It is reported among the nations—and Geshem says it is true—that you and the Jews are planning to revolt, and therefore you are building the wall. Moreover, according to these reports you are about to become their king and have even appointed prophets to make this proclamation about you in Jerusalem: 'There is a king in Judah!' Now this report will get back to the king; so come, let us confer together."

We have words for this: political "hardball"; something from the experienced campaigner's bag of "dirty tricks."

It was not new in substance, of course. It was a revival of the charge made earlier: "What is this you are doing? . . . Are you rebelling against the king?" (Neh. 2:19). What made it new (and "dirty") was the *open* letter that suggested it. An open letter would have been a read letter. It would have been read scores of times during its progress from Samaria to Jerusalem, and the message would already have been repeated widely by the time Nehemiah received the accusation. In other words, as in the case of all gossip, the damage was already done.

When rumors spread, the subject of the talk gets hurt. Even if the rumor is later proven false, the victim of gossip inevitably suffers.

Moreover, the letter was a threat to hurt Nehemiah even more. For when Sanballat said, "This report will get back to the king; so come, let us confer together" (v. 7), he was not offering to help, as his words seemed to indicate. He was actually threatening to report Nehemiah to Artaxerxes if Nehemiah refused to cooperate. In fact, it was worse than that. The report was already abroad. Now Sanballat was threatening to endorse it officially.

What is a leader to do in such circumstances? Well, if ever a leader needs inner strength, it is in such cases. His own heart must be pure, first of all. If Nehemiah had actually been planning to become king and lead a revolt, he would have been weak-kneed with indecision. A leader needs inner strength to act decisively.

Look what he did. As soon as Nehemiah heard the report, he replied immediately to Sanballat: "Nothing like what you are saying is happening; you are just making it up out of your head" (v. 8). He adds in his memoirs,

"They were all trying to frighten us, thinking, 'Their hands will get too weak for the work, and it will not be completed'" (v. 9).

We have a contemporary but contrary example of this in the 1988 presidential election between Vice President George Bush and Massachusetts Governor Michael Dukakis. After he lost the election and was asked what he considered the reasons for his failure, Dukakis replied by blaming the Bush campaign for its personal attacks on him. He said, "Our mistake was not replying to those false accusations immediately." Whether or not the attacks were fair is something people will judge in different ways, depending on their political loyalties. But the principle is a valid one. The only way to handle a false rumor is by denying it immediately, which is what Nehemiah did.

He did something else too. He prayed (v. 9). Why? Because although he denied Sanballat's false rumor as directly and emphatically as possible, he did not know whether his denial would be believed or whether he would survive the assault. Sanballat might have denounced him to Artaxerxes, supporting the rumor. Artaxerxes might have believed Sanballat. Nehemiah might have been recalled and beheaded. So he turned to his only true source of strength, as he was accustomed to do.

"Now strengthen my hands," Nehemiah prayed.

In the final analysis, that is all we can do also. We must commit our case to God and press forward.

Where did Nehemiah get his inner strength? Obviously from his relationship with God. And if it came from God in Nehemiah's case, it can come from God for us as well.

Cyril Barber cites Maurice E. Wagner as having said it this way:

> Personal security . . . comes from our relationship to the three Persons of the Godhead. Our relationship to God the Father gives us a sense of *belonging*. We are members of his family and are secure in our Father-child relationship. Our union with Christ the Son gives us a sense of *worth*. God loved us so much that he sent his son to die for our sins. With our redemption accomplished, God has made us joint heirs with Christ. This shows our value. Finally, the Holy Spirit's indwelling empowers us. We are made equal to every task (i.e., we are *competent*).[3]

A person whose life is anchored on these three foundational relationships will be able to stand against all hostile attacks.

Opposition by Intimidation

The final form of opposition was outright intimidation. Like the others, it too was subtle. Apparently, a man who was regarded as a prophet sent for Nehemiah. His name was Shemaiah. Nehemiah tells us that Shemaiah was shut up in his house, though we do not know why. It could have been because of ill health or a vow, but in view of what follows, it was probably because of pretended fear on his part. Whatever the immediate cause, the underlying reason was a carefully designed ruse to discredit Nehemiah. When Nehemiah accepted the invitation and went to see him, Shemaiah said, "Let us meet in the house of God, inside the temple, and let us close the temple doors, because men are coming to kill you—by night they are coming to kill you" (v. 10).

There are several things to notice about this suggestion. First, although it is not very apparent in our English translations, it was dressed up as an oracle and presented to Nehemiah as a revelation from God. Several of the more scholarly translations handle it this way. The Jerusalem Bible sets it out in separate lines, ending with this couplet:

> for they are coming to kill you,
> they are coming to kill you tonight.[4]
>
> Nehemiah 6:10

Second, look at the nature of this "surprise" attack. It was a temptation for Nehemiah to do two wrong things: (1) to put his own safety ahead of the work and (2) to break God's law in order to save his life.

This deserves an explanation. When Shemaiah suggested that he and Nehemiah flee to the "temple" to save themselves, the term he used means "the Holy Place" and not just the temple enclosure. This was a pagan suggestion, for it was a pagan belief, not a Jewish one, that a person could be spared punishment for a crime by fleeing to one of the heathen temples and living there, even if guilty of something quite serious. The Jews had a similar device in the six cities of refuge (cf. Deut. 19:1–13; Josh. 20:1–9), though these were for people guilty only of *unintentional* homicide, not murder. There was no provision for help linked to the Jewish temple. Shemaiah was speaking as a pagan at this point.

Moreover, he was suggesting something that was contrary to the Old Testament's teaching. Nehemiah was a layman, and laymen were not allowed into the inner portions of the temple (Num. 18:7). King Uzziah, who violated that prohibition, had been fortunate to escape with no more than leprosy (2 Chron. 26:16–21). If Nehemiah had succumbed to Shemaiah's artful suggestions, he would have been seriously compromised and might even have lost his life.

The first time we read Nehemiah's response, we are tempted to think of it as the reply of a forceful and perhaps even arrogant man: "Should a man like me run away? Or should one like me go into the temple to save his life? I will not go!" (v. 11). But when we read the rest of what Nehemiah says, we understand that his reply involves much more than his own self-esteem. He says several things, including the following: (1) that having agreed to do what Shemaiah suggested would have been sin on his part (v. 13) and (2) that God had not sent Shemaiah (v. 12). How did he know this? Obviously, because he knew the Old Testament forbade a layman to enter the Holy Place. He knew that God had not sent Shemaiah, because God had given the Old Testament, and the God who forbids us from doing one thing in one place does not contradict himself by telling us to do it in another. He is at all times consistent.

If we could learn that, it would save us much trouble. Normally, instead of obeying God, we disobey him and assume that God will therefore change his mind and alter his requirement. But he does not, and we do not triumph in the situation, as Nehemiah did. Cyril Barber writes that Nehemiah triumphed, "not by breaking God's law to escape assassination, but by keeping it!"[5]

"The Secret of [His] Success"

Some time ago actor Michael J. Fox starred in a movie about New York business empires entitled *The Secret of My Success.* In these first chapters of Nehemiah, we learn something much more important than the secret of success in business. We learn the secret of Nehemiah's success as a leader and man of God. This is a place to review these five leadership characteristics.

1. Nehemiah's closeness to God and his prayerfulness. Nothing is more characteristic of Nehemiah than his closeness to God, expressed most often by his praying to God on all occasions. We have seen it before. We see it two more times in this chapter (vv. 9, 14). Nehemiah saw everything that happened to him within a spiritual framework.

2. Nehemiah's sense of calling to a task. In secular terms, it is a matter of objectives. Robert Townsend, author of *Up the Organization* and *Further Up the Organization,* writes that "one of the important functions of a leader is to make the organization concentrate on its objectives."[6] He cites the Roman senator Cato, who, by constantly repeating the three words *delenda est Carthago* ("Carthage must be destroyed"), eventually moved the Roman Empire to strike and destroy its North African rival.[7] Nehemiah had a strong sense of his one great objective, which was to rebuild the wall, but it went beyond that. Above all, he knew himself to be God's man and to have a call to God's service.

3. Nehemiah's self-awareness and knowledge of his own worth. This was not a vain self-assessment. The gifts Nehemiah had were from God; he would not have had them otherwise. He knew that he had these gifts and was not the least bit overawed by the task he was given or intimidated by his adversaries. We should have an equally strong sense of personal value. We should know that we are equipped by God for whatever task he has for us.

4. Nehemiah's extraordinary discernment. Nehemiah also showed great discernment. He was able to detect in every subterfuge of the enemy exactly what was going on. Where did he get such discernment? Some of it may have been a natural gift, of course, but a large part of it must have come from his spiritual experience and understanding.

Do you remember those words spoken about Jesus near the beginning of John's Gospel? Jesus had cleansed the temple and was creating a great stir. Many who saw his miracles were believing on him. "But," we are told, "Jesus would not entrust himself to them, for he knew all men. He did not need man's testimony about man, for he knew what was in a man" (John 2:24–25). Jesus did not have exalted opinions of human beings. Therefore, he was able to keep his perspective and pursue his own course. It was the same with Nehemiah. He knew what was in man. Therefore, he was not beguiled even by the most subtle devices of his enemies. He was able to focus on the real issues and priorities.

5. *Nehemiah's great courage.* We must not forget this element, for many people have had other important gifts and yet have failed in times of testing because of a lack of courage. "Should a man like me run away?" Nehemiah asked (6:11). John White comments, "The words echo across the centuries to us. Like Nehemiah we live in days when we must let our courage be seen by the way we act and speak. It will help us, perhaps, to realize that true courage does not consist in the absence of fear but in doing what God wants even when we are afraid, disturbed and hurt."[8]

Who is not afraid at times? Who is not disturbed? Who is not hurt? We all are. Yet it is precisely when we yield those fears to God and press on that we show leadership.

8

The Completion of the Wall

Nehemiah 6:15–7:73

So the wall was completed on the twenty-fifth of Elul, in fifty-two days. When all our enemies heard about this, all the surrounding nations were afraid and lost their self-confidence, because they realized that this work had been done with the help of our God. . . .

After the wall had been rebuilt and I had set the doors in place, the gatekeepers and the singers and the Levites were appointed. I put in charge of Jerusalem my brother Hanani, along with Hananiah the commander of the citadel, because he was a man of integrity and feared God more than most men do. I said to them, "The gates of Jerusalem are not to be opened until the sun is hot. While the gatekeepers are still on duty, have them shut the doors and bar them. Also appoint residents of Jerusalem as guards, some at their posts and some near their own houses."

Nehemiah 6:15–16; 7:1–3

Nobody who watched the 1988 Summer Olympic Games from Seoul, Korea, will ever forget Greg Louganis. Already the best diver in the world, Louganis came to Seoul to do what no Olympic competitor had ever done before: to win both the springboard and platform competitions in two consecutive Olympics. He had won both in Los Angeles in 1984.

Louganis was used to obstacles. He was born out of wedlock, and though he had been adopted by a very supportive family, he nevertheless had for years fought a sense of not belonging. He was shy. Moreover, as the family later discovered, Greg suffered from dyslexia, which in his grade school and high school days led him to think he was mentally handicapped. It was not until his first year at the University of Miami that he identified his problem.

Louganis reacted to these obstacles by pouring his energy into diving, where his natural skills and hard work gradually took him to the top of the sport. By the time he reached the 1988 Olympics, he had already won forty-three national diving titles, six Pan American gold medals, and five world championships.

It was difficult in Seoul. Now almost thirty, Greg was the oldest of the divers, and he was being pressed by a new generation of athletes, most of whom had learned many of their skills by watching him—including the difficult three-and-one-half reverse somersault tuck, which he had invented. The three-and-one-half reverse tuck was so difficult that it had killed a Soviet diver in Canada in 1983. The Russian had struck his head on the diving platform and died from a brain hemorrhage a week later.

In Seoul, Louganis quickly won the springboard competition. However, during the trials for the platform competition, his head hit the platform on the same dive that had killed the Russian athlete. He made the finals due to his earlier high scores, but everyone wondered if, after his accident, he would be able to dive well and defeat the unusually fierce competition. In the finals, the contest came down to the final dive, Louganis's own reverse somersault. His chief competitor, a young Chinese diver, was leading. Back arched and knees flexed, Louganis launched himself high into the air, curled into a tight ball, and spun backward toward the crystal blue water thirty-three feet below. The dive was sensational, and he won the platform competition by a bare fraction of a point.

"You did it, buddy," viewers heard his coach say. And indeed he had.

What a thrill to tackle something extremely difficult and keep at it until you reach a triumphant conclusion.

"So the Wall Was Completed"

That is what Nehemiah did, and that is why it remains thrilling to read his story even today.

Nehemiah had come to Jerusalem from Susa with a single-minded objective: to rebuild the massive but ruined wall of Jerusalem. He was beset by obstacles. First, he had to gain permission from the Babylonian emperor Artaxerxes, which meant getting him to reverse an earlier state policy against rebuilding the Jewish capital. Once in Jerusalem, Nehemiah had to devise a plan for accomplishing his task and then find ways to motivate the people to tackle it. When the work got started, he was opposed by the governors of the surrounding provinces and by injustices within Israel. Nehemiah's enemies tried to stop the work by ridicule, threat of violence, intrigue, harmful rumors, and intimidation. His wealthier countrymen almost scuttled it by their oppression of the poor.

But Nehemiah pressed on. So great was the task and so great its accomplishment that we can hardly miss the thrill of the superb understatement in verse 15: "So the wall was completed on the twenty-fifth of Elul, in fifty-two days."

Nehemiah had received his brother's report about Jerusalem when he was in Susa in the month of Kislev, in the winter of 444 BC. Nehemiah received permission to go to Jerusalem in the month of Nisan, our April. Preparation and travel took time, so he arrived in Jerusalem and began the work on what we would call August 1. Now, fifty-two days later, on September 21, the reconstruction of the massive wall was done—one and a half to two and a half miles of masonry. From the time he had first heard about the problem when he was in Susa until the wall was finished was only nine months. The construction was completed within two months of his arrival in the city.

What perseverance! What courage! Cyril J. Barber writes:

> His was the faith that moves mountains. His confidence in God gave him the courage to plod on in spite of the clouds of opposition that gathered around him. He boldly championed the cause of right and scorned the things that would inspire fear. Nehemiah's courage helped him attain new heights of achievement. Armed with this fortitude, he turned obstacles into opportunities, and outward trials into personal triumphs.[1]

If ever there was a time when Nehemiah could have been tempted to sit back and take credit for his success, it was when the wall was completed. But he did not. What he did do shows his greatness.

First, toward the end of chapter 6 we learn that Nehemiah gave glory to God. He says, "When all our enemies heard about this, all the surrounding nations were afraid and lost their self-confidence, because they realized that this work had been done with the help of our God" (v. 16).

Since Nehemiah had come from the winter capital of Babylon, I cannot help but think of the contrasting words of that earlier Babylonian king, Nebuchadnezzar, who had conquered Jerusalem. Nebuchadnezzar was proud of his accomplishments, and one day, when he was walking on the roof of his royal place in Babylon, he looked out over the city and said, "Is not this the great Babylon I have built as the royal residence, by my mighty power and for the glory of my majesty?" (Dan. 4:30). It was the exact opposite of what Nehemiah said. Nehemiah gave glory to God for his achievement.

Therefore, Nehemiah prospered and Nebuchadnezzar was judged. The latter's story continues:

> The words were still on his lips when a voice came from heaven, "This is what is decreed for you, King Nebuchadnezzar: Your royal authority has been taken from you. You will be driven away from people and will live with the wild animals; you will eat grass like cattle. Seven times will pass by for you until you acknowledge that the Most High is sovereign over the kingdoms of men and gives them to anyone he wishes."
>
> Daniel 4:31–32

Immediately, Nebuchadnezzar became irrational and was driven out of the palace to live with the cattle in the fields until his reason was restored to him by God years later.

Why is it that so many people will acknowledge God and even pray to him regularly and fervently on their way up the long ladder of success, but once they reach that pinnacle, they forget their religion and regard success as their own exclusive achievement? It is inexplicable, unless the reason is that they conveniently "forget" God so they can indulge themselves without any higher responsibility.

Nehemiah did not do this. He remembered God and so retained his usefulness to God beyond the accomplishment of his initial objective. That is why the book does not end with chapter 6; the second half is filled with equally remarkable achievements.

Second, as Nehemiah reports his achievement, he does not allow success to blind him to his continuing problems. Or, to put it another way, he does not pretend his success is greater than it really is. Many people do this. They are so pleased with their success that they will not admit any failures or imperfections. Nehemiah does admit them. In fact, this is the way chapter 6 ends (vv. 17–19):

> Also, in those days the nobles of Judah were sending many letters to Tobiah, and replies from Tobiah kept coming to them. For many in Judah were under oath to him, since he was son-in-law to Shecaniah son of Arah, and his son Jehohanan had married the daughter of Meshullam son of Berekiah. Moreover, they kept reporting to me his good deeds and then telling him what I said. And Tobiah sent letters to intimidate me.

We are probably not able to understand fully what is going on in this report. But we can tell that it is at least a realistic admission by Nehemiah of his continuing problems. Tobiah had been a source of opposition all along. We are going to find him causing trouble even at the very end of the book (in chap. 13). His opposition was particularly troublesome for three reasons: (1) he was a Jew, like Nehemiah, (2) he had profitable trading agreements with the wealthier classes in Jerusalem (this is what the words *under oath* seem to refer to), and (3) he was linked to the wealthier Jewish families by marriage. When we remember that it was these very families that had been oppressing the poor and that Nehemiah had forced to back down, return what they had extorted, and abandon their policies, we can understand how these people might well have continued to resent Nehemiah despite their public change of heart and how Tobiah might have had strong allies in them. These people were no doubt all drawing together, planning for the day when they would have the upper hand in Judah once again.

Does this apply to us? It does indeed. We live in a sinful and wicked world, and our calling to live and work for the Lord Jesus Christ in that world is never ended. We need to remember that, especially when we have achieved some important objective.

Consolidation or Preparation?

In the seventh chapter of Nehemiah, we come to another list of names, similar to the list of the builders of the wall in chapter 3. But this list is even sparser in information than the earlier one. In fact, it is really only a census from the archives. Nehemiah did not write it. We know this because it is almost identical to the list recorded by Ezra in the second chapter of the book by his name.[2] Why is this list here, particularly since it has already appeared in Ezra? Or, to ask the question in a different way, are we to take chapter 7 as a wrap-up and consolidation of the task of rebuilding, which we have in the first six chapters of Nehemiah, or as an introduction to the achievements of the book's second half?

The answer is, probably both. In Ezra the list is included to answer the question "Who is a true Jew?" It is what we would expect a scribe and religious leader like Ezra to be asking. In Nehemiah the list serves another purpose. Now that the wall has been built, Nehemiah is going to turn his attention to repopulating and revitalizing the city. His census is a follow-up on his first effort as well as preparation for what is to come.

How do we study this chapter? Since it contains more than just the census, I suggest that these additional elements are the clue to understanding it. The three actions described consolidate the work and prepare for the coming revitalization of Jerusalem.

Key Appointments

Nehemiah's first step after having completed the rebuilding of the wall was to make a few key appointments. The first verses of chapter 7 tell us about three general categories of appointments (gatekeepers, singers, and Levites) and two specific ones: his brother Hanani as the civil leader of Jerusalem (Nehemiah was governor of the province) and Hananiah as the military commander in charge of Jerusalem's new defenses. The text says, "After the wall had been rebuilt and I had set the doors in place, the gate-keepers and the singers and the Levites were appointed. I put in charge of Jerusalem my brother Hanani, along with Hananiah the commander of the citadel, because he was a man of integrity and feared God more than most men do" (Neh. 7:1–2).

What is happening here? The answer is something well known in the business world. When an executive is assigned a difficult job, perhaps to reorganize a declining company or to develop a new organization, the wise leader will often have a large number of people report to him directly. He wants to keep in the closest possible contact with what is happening. At this stage, his organizational chart might look like this:

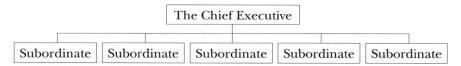

However, if the company or project begins to function efficiently, the executive may then withdraw from much of the hands-on management and work increasingly through other people, who in turn will manage others. At this stage, the organizational chart will resemble the more traditional pyramid:

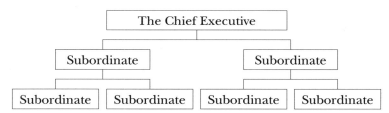

So far as Jerusalem was concerned, Nehemiah was now prepared to work through two chief operating officers: Hanani, the civic leader (Nehemiah's equivalent of a mayor), and Hananiah, the military leader (Nehemiah's equivalent of what for us would be the chief of police).

Some writers have accused Nehemiah of nepotism in these appointments since Hanani is identified as his "brother," while others, trying to protect Nehemiah's reputation, have argued that Hanani was his brother only in the sense of being a fellow Jew. But they were all Jews. That is what the list in chapter 7 is about. So if Hanani is called Nehemiah's brother, it must be because he really was Nehemiah's flesh-and-blood brother. That might even have been the reason Hanani was the one chosen to make the journey to Susa to see Nehemiah at the beginning of the story (Neh. 1:1–2); he would have been certain of gaining access to him. Was this nepotism, then? No. It was simply a case of Nehemiah's picking the best and most loyal man for the job. Hanani had already demonstrated concern for the city's welfare by making the long trip to Babylon to rouse Nehemiah. Now he could be counted on to be loyal to him. Loyalty was an important matter at the time when the intrigue described in Nehemiah 6:17–19 was still going on. Nehemiah needed to guard against treachery.

Theodore Roosevelt, a remarkable American president, said to leaders, "The best executive is the one who has sense enough to pick good men to do what he wants done, and self-restraint enough to keep from meddling with them while they do it."[3]

There is one more factor in Nehemiah's appointment of key leaders we need to look at before we go on. It is his provision of adequate guidelines for them (Neh. 7:3). Nehemiah understood the need for strong men in key posts. He was willing to let them do their jobs without meddling; we are going to see more of this in the second half of the book. But this does not mean he neglected to give them direction. We would call it job descriptions, written objectives, and performance standards. In Nehemiah's terms, it is what we find in verse 3: "I said to them, 'The gates of Jerusalem are not to be opened until the sun is hot. While the gatekeepers are still on duty, have them shut the doors and bar them. Also appoint residents of Jerusalem as guards, some at their posts and some near their own houses.'" These are specific directives, and we can assume there were others like them.

Numbering the People

The largest part of chapter 7 is the "extract from the archives" (from Ezra), as I pointed out earlier. It must have been regarded as an important document since it is found not only here and in Ezra 2 but in the apocryphal book of 1 Esdras also. We have already seen that its presence in Nehemiah has an entirely different purpose than in the book of his predecessor. Ezra's question was religious: Who among the body of returned exiles were Jews? In Nehemiah the object is secular. The question is this: Who is available to repopulate and revitalize the city? The document contains nine categories.

1. The original leaders (vv. 6–7). We do not know who all these persons were, but at least the first two are well known and important. They are Zerubbabel the civil leader and Jeshua (or Joshua) the religious leader, who together brought the first body of exiles to Judah after Cyrus permitted their return. These leaders figure strongly in two of the last books of the Old Testament, the minor prophets Haggai and Zechariah. Zerubbabel was of the royal line of Judah. From Joshua there descended fourteen successive generations of high priests.

2. Jews who were laymen (vv. 8–38). This is a long and numerically significant list, as might be expected. It is in two parts. The first part lists eighteen individuals from whom the then-living descendants came. The second part lists twenty towns in which the returning exiles settled. The introduction to the census suggests that these were the towns from which the families of these people had come originally.

3. Priests (vv. 39–42). The priests were the descendants of Aaron, Moses's brother. They were responsible for the service of the great temple altar and aspects of the feasts. David had organized the priests into twenty-four families, each responsible for a two- or three-week tour of temple duty. Nehemiah's list mentions only four of these families, presumably the only ones who returned. According to the Talmud, these were later reorganized into a new set of twenty-four rotation groups using the original Davidic names (cf. Tosephta, ii, I, 216). Nehemiah lists just over four thousand priests—about one-tenth of the total census.

4. Levites (v. 43). Levites were the descendants of Levi, one of the original twelve patriarchs. Levites also served in rotation, and their job was to assist the priests descended from Aaron. Surprisingly, a very small number is listed, meaning that only a minority of the Levites had returned from Babylon.[4]

5. Singers (v. 44). The singers, like the gatekeepers who follow, were taken from among the Levites. Their task was to assist in the temple worship (cf. 2 Chron. 25–26).

6. Gatekeepers (v. 45). The Levites, singers, and gatekeepers were the categories of temple staff appointed by Nehemiah, according to verse 1. They were not the people mentioned by name here, of course; they were from among their descendants.

7. Temple servants (vv. 46–56). Temple servants were assistants to the Levites, just as Levites were assistants to the descendants of Aaron. The Gibeonites had been appointed to this role after they had deceived the Israelites at the time of the conquest. In fact, these actually might have been their descendants, now incorporated into the nation by circumcision.

8. The descendants of the servants of Solomon (vv. 57–60). This group was closely linked to the previous one, a common total serving for both groups.

9. Those whose ancestry was questionable (vv. 61–65). These were in two categories: laymen and those who claimed to be priests. The situation of the priests was most serious since it involved matters of ritual purity and contamination for the whole people. A decision was made to exclude these persons from priestly functions until their case could be decided by submitting it to a sacred casting of lots known as the Urim and Thummim.

The census ends with the total number of Jews, to which are added a number of other totals, including those of servants, singers, and animals.

Providing for the Temple

The final action taken by Nehemiah in his attempt to consolidate his earlier work and prepare for the tasks to come was to provide for those who would now be working in the temple. We find this in the next verses of the chapter (vv. 70–72):

> Some of the heads of the families contributed to the work. The governor gave to the treasury 1,000 drachmas of gold, 50 bowls and 530 garments for priests. Some of the heads of the families gave to the treasury for the work 20,000 drachmas of gold and 2,200 minas of silver. The total given by the rest of the people was 20,000 drachmas of gold, 2,000 minas of silver and 67 garments for priests.

The chapter ends by noting, "The priests, the Levites, the gatekeepers, the singers and the temple servants, along with certain of the people and the rest of the Israelites, settled in their own towns" (v. 73).

We know that a number of the wealthier Jewish families were teamed up with Tobiah, since Nehemiah says so. They would be hostile to Nehemiah's plans and reforms. But in fairness to the rich, it needs to be noted that not all were opposed to Nehemiah. Otherwise, where would the considerable wealth mentioned in verses 70–72 have come from? It is difficult to evaluate the true purchasing power of sums of ancient money, but if the notes in the New International Version are correct (they represent only the best judgment of scholars), the families of Israel gave gold and silver worth, in today's currency, more than $5 million. That made a considerable endowment for the temple service, and Nehemiah's care to provide it shows that although he was a layman, he cared not only for secular matters but for the spiritual well-being of the people as well. In fact, this is what follows in the second half of his memoir.

We have already seen many great traits of leadership in Nehemiah. Here we see four more. First, he realized the need for new leaders and worked to seek out and appoint them. Second, he knew that new leaders needed clear and proper guidelines to be effective. Although he was delegating the work, he was still in charge. Third, he knew that God's work must be supported financially. Finally, he knew that:

> Unless the LORD builds the house,
>   its builders labor in vain.
> Unless the LORD watches over the city,
>   The watchmen stand guard in vain.
>
>   Psalm 127:1

It is a lesson every true leader needs to learn, in his personal life and in what he seeks to accomplish.

PART 2

Rebuilding the Nation

9

The Sixth Dynamic:
A Nation under God, Part 1

Nehemiah 7:73–8:18

When the seventh month came and the Israelites had settled in their towns, all the people assembled as one man in the square before the Water Gate. They told Ezra the scribe to bring out the Book of the Law of Moses, which the LORD had commanded for Israel.

So on the first day of the seventh month Ezra the priest brought the Law before the assembly, which was made up of men and women and all who were able to understand. He read it aloud from daybreak till noon as he faced the square before the Water Gate in the presence of the men, women and others who could understand. And all the people listened attentively to the Book of the Law.

Ezra the scribe stood on a high wooden platform built for the occasion. Beside him on his right stood Mattithiah, Shema, Anaiah, Uriah, Hilkiah and Maaseiah; and on his left were Pedaiah, Mishael, Malkijah, Hashum, Hashbaddanah, Zechariah and Meshullam.

Ezra opened the book. All the people could see him because he was standing above them; and as he opened it, the people all stood up. Ezra praised the LORD, the great God; and all the people lifted their hands and responded, "Amen! Amen!" Then they bowed down and worshiped the LORD with their faces to the ground.

The Levites—Jeshua, Bani, Sherebiah, Jamin, Akkub, Shabbethai, Hodiah, Maaseiah, Kelita, Azariah, Jozabad, Hanan and Pelaiah—instructed the people in the Law while the people were standing there. They read from the Book of the Law of God, making it clear and giving the meaning so that the people would understand what was being read. . . .

Day after day, from the first day to the last, Ezra read from the Book of the Law of God. They celebrated the feast for seven days, and on the eighth day, in accordance with the regulation, there was an assembly.

Nehemiah 8:1–8, 18

Anyone who is concerned about the proper impact of Christianity upon a nation knows the name of William Wilberforce, the power behind the abolition of slavery in the British Empire in the year 1807. Wilberforce was elected to Parliament from the county of Hull in 1780 at the age of twenty-one. He was converted to Christ in 1785 through the witness of his old schoolmaster from Hull, Isaac Milner. Shortly after that, partly through the influence of the converted former slave trader John Newton and partly through others, Wilberforce began his long campaign against slavery.

Wilberforce's first parliamentary bill was to "discuss" abolition. It was introduced in the House of Commons by his friend Prime Minister William Pitt in 1788, and it passed. But when the bill came up for discussion at the next session of Parliament in 1789, it was hotly opposed by the commercial lobby that backed slavery, and the move to limit the abuse was defeated.

"Humanity is a private feeling, not a public principle to act upon," said the influential Earl of Abingdon.

"Things have come to a pretty pass when religion is allowed to invade public life," said Lord Melbourne.

In 1791 Wilberforce, now backed by a coalition of like-minded men known as the Clapham Sect, tried again, but again he was defeated. It was the same in 1792. There were times when public opinion ran in Wilberforce's favor. At other times, as in the eyes of the French Revolution, opinion was against any change at all. After the fall of Robespierre in France in 1796, the mood of the country turned toward abolition, but when the abolition bill reached the House of Commons in that year, it was again defeated.

So also in 1798, 1799, 1800, and 1801.

It was not until February 4, 1807, that the abolition document finally passed the House of Lords, and not until February 22, 1807, that it passed the Commons. Nineteen years had gone by. Men had grown old in the cause. Some had died. Yet when news of the abolition of the slave trade reached Wilberforce late on the evening of February 22, the reformer looked into the face of his old friend and fellow abolitionist Henry Thorton and said, "Well, Henry, what shall we abolish next?"[1]

Rebuilding the Nation

The situation must have been the same for Nehemiah, governor of Jerusalem, after he had succeeded in rebuilding Jerusalem's great wall. Nehemiah had come to Jerusalem to do that, and so intent had he been on achieving that single great objective that those looking on might have imagined that rebuilding the wall was all he had in mind.

How wrong they would have been! Nehemiah had indeed come to Jerusalem to rebuild the wall, and he had been successful in doing it. But we discover now that the rebuilding was far from all he had in mind. Nehemiah wanted to rebuild the wall, but beyond that objective he had the far more significant objective of rebuilding the nation.

One commentator has written:

> His commission from God was far more comprehensive than that of merely rebuilding the defenses of Jerusalem. The wall was merely the first step in the rebuilding of a nation. And along with Ezra, Nehemiah was to lay foundations for national reforms that would continue to make their impact for more than four centuries—until the coming of Christ.[2]

In one sense, Nehemiah's shift from the single-minded effort to rebuild the wall to his concern for the nation comes as a surprise to the reader. He has not mentioned anything beyond the walls up to this point. Still, we have been prepared by the list of those then living in the land (chap. 7). As I pointed out in the last chapter, Nehemiah 7 serves two purposes. It is a consolidation of the first half of the book, listing those who were available to live in the now protected city. But it is also a preparation for the spiritual renewal of the nation that lay ahead. It alerts us to the fact that Nehemiah had already begun to shift to this objective.

We see this shift in another way as well, although it is not quite so easy to know what this change means. Up to this point, Nehemiah has been writing in the first person. With the start of chapter 8, this changes. Here the narrative shifts to the third person, and the first-person narration does not resume until the start of the account of the dedication of the walls in Nehemiah 12:27.

This seems to mean that Nehemiah was aware that the second stage of the work, though envisioned by him, was not his concern alone. He cared about the nation's spiritual renewal, but this was a matter to be pursued by Ezra, the spiritual head of the people, more than by himself. So the leadership in the movement for renewal passed to the hands of Ezra, though Nehemiah was still very much involved.

In the second half of the book, we find the following key elements: (1) a revival of the people through a reading of the Law, confession of sin, and a renewal of the covenant (chaps. 8–10); (2) the repopulation of Jerusalem

(11:1–12:26); and (3) the final, joyous dedication of the walls (12:27–47). As a postscript, chapter 13 details Nehemiah's final reforms.

It is important to note something else as we begin this new section. In our study of this book, we have been dealing with a number of leadership dynamics apparent in Nehemiah. We have already seen five: (1) the leader and God, (2) the leader and his superior or superiors, (3) the leader and his subordinates, (4) the leader and the task, and (5) the leader and opposition. At this point we see a sixth dynamic, which is the leader and the nation. This is important because it is a way of saying that however isolated our particular task or challenge may be, it is nevertheless always part of a greater whole, since we are citizens of a nation and what we do affect the larger body. We need to care for it as well.

Reading God's Word First

In the eighth chapter of Nehemiah, we see the starting point for any true national renewal. It is the Word of God.

Verses 2–12 tell of a great public assembly in which Ezra the priest read the Law of God to the people and of how they were affected by it. The people came to the city from the surrounding countryside, gathered in the large public square before the Water Gate on Jerusalem's eastern side, and listened to Ezra. Ezra mounted a large wooden platform that had been erected for just this occasion, and there, flanked by thirteen of the most prominent Levites, he read from the book of the Law (the Pentateuch or "the first five books") from early morning until noon—about six hours.

The people showed extraordinary reverence for the Law, for they rose in respectful silence when Ezra opened the scroll. When he prayed, they responded, "Amen! Amen!" and worshiped God. As the account unfolds, we discover that the reading of God's Law led to national revival.

That is what we need in the United States. Instead of honoring the Word of God and hungering after it as the people of Judah did in the days of Nehemiah and Ezra, our country seems intent on doing everything possible to keep the Bible and even religion itself from public life. It is strange that this should be so, since our country was founded with a conscious attention to and respect for biblical principles.

We have been told that our founding fathers were for the most part unbelievers or at best deists. While there is some truth to that, it is also a distortion.

Thomas Jefferson (1743–1826) was a deist, but that does not mean he utterly discounted the Bible. On the contrary, he said, "The Bible is the cornerstone of liberty."[3]

Benjamin Franklin (1706–1790) was a skeptical unbeliever, but he believed in prayer. He inaugurated the practice of prayer before deliberation, which still prevails in Congress.

George Washington (1732–1799) gave strong testimony of faith. In a small prayer book composed when he was about twenty years old, Washington wrote:

> O most glorious God . . . remember that I am but dust, and remit my transgressions, negligences and ignorances, and cover them all with the absolute obedience of thy dear Son, that those sacrifices (of sin, praise and thanksgiving) which I have offered may be accepted by thee, in and for the sacrifice of Jesus Christ offered upon the cross for me. . . . Direct my thoughts, words and work; wash away my sin in the immaculate blood of the Lamb; and purge my heart by the Holy Spirit.[4]

John Witherspoon (1723–1794), president of the College of New Jersey (now Princeton) and the only clergyman to sign the Declaration of Independence, wrote, "He is the best friend to American liberty who is most sincere and active in promoting true and undefiled religion."[5]

Andrew Jackson (1767–1845), seventh president of the United States, said, "The Bible is the rock on which our Republic rests."[6]

Daniel Webster (1782–1852), the great American statesman and orator, said, "There is no solid basis for civilization but in the Word of God. If we are to abide by the principles taught in the Bible, our country will go on prospering. . . . The Bible is a book . . . which teaches man his own individual responsibility, his own dignity, and his equality with his fellowman."[7]

William McKinley (1843–1901), twenty-fifth president of the United States, declared, "The more profoundly we study this wonderful Book, and the more closely we observe its precepts, the better citizens we will become and the higher will be the destiny of our nation."[8]

Each of these men, though possessing various degrees of spiritual understanding and differing in their ecclesiastical traditions, recognized that a nation is only as strong as its underlying faith in God and that the Bible is essential for survival.

How far away from that we have fallen! How much we need to rediscover Scripture!

First Steps to Revival

If we are to see a spiritual recovery in our land today, it will be helpful to review the steps to revival as revealed in the following activities.

1. Ezra began by prayer (v. 6). This is the first appearance of Ezra in Nehemiah (cf. v. 1), and his prayer preceding his reading of the Law, which is not even recorded, might be considered merely a formal invocation. This would be wrong, however. Ezra's appearance is significant, and his prayer was more than merely formal, as the response of the people shows.

What did Ezra's prayer accomplish? It seems to have accomplished two things. First, it established the sense among the people that what was to follow—the reading of the Law—was no mere civil matter but had to do with God. A number of commentators have pointed out the importance of the way the book of the Law is introduced: "The Book of the Law of Moses, which the LORD had commanded for Israel" (v. 1). That makes two significant points. First, the Law was already a recognized entity among the people. It was not something that was still in the process of evolving or being developed, which is what the higher critics of the Old Testament have argued. Second, it was already invested with complete divine authority. It was not merely a human book. It was from God, and it was to be revered as such. Ezra acknowledged this and reminded the people of it when he began this historic reading of the Old Testament with prayer.

Second, Ezra's prayer awakened the people's anticipation of what God might do among them. Prayer should always do this, for prayer is approaching God and asking things of and receiving things from him. (It is also praise, confession, and thanksgiving. Those elements are present even in this story. But it is also asking and expecting.) Certainly the people were not wrong to be in an expectant frame of mind on this occasion.

2. Ezra read the Word of God (v. 3). Much was done to raise the Bible in the people's thinking. Prayer was part of it. But so were the elevated platform from which Ezra read and the way Ezra was flanked by the thirteen Levites whose names are recorded in verse 4. Perhaps most important is the fact that Ezra read from the Law for six hours.

I wonder if we have a similar respect for God's Word and if we think of it as highly. I notice that the people stood when Ezra opened the scroll, and that reminds me of something that is still practiced in many churches in Scotland. It is customary in Scottish churches for the service to begin by the entrance of a man called the beadle. He enters carrying the Bible, which he places on the church's pulpit and then opens to the day's reading, after which he escorts the minister to the pulpit. The important thing about this ceremony is that the people stand when the beadle enters with the Bible, and they remain standing until it is opened and the minister has taken his place behind it with the implied but obvious assignment to expound it. Only after that do the people resume their places.

When the International Council on Biblical Inerrancy held its first large lay "Congress on the Bible" in San Diego in 1982, we tried to introduce this custom to American churches by having each of our public sessions begin in that way. So far as I know, the ceremony did not catch on, but it was impressive in San Diego, as each time the Bible was brought in, more than three thousand people rose and then were seated.

Some would call this bibliolatry, the worship of a book, but it is no such thing. It is acknowledgment of what the Bible is: the very Word of God. It is a proper heart respect that prepares the worshiper for hearing it expounded.

3. The explanation of God's Word (vv. 7–8). One of the most important parts of Nehemiah is the statement in verses 7 and 8 of this chapter that the reading of the Law was accompanied by interpretation or explanation. The text says, "The Levites—Jeshua, Bani, Sherebiah, Jamin, Akkub, Shabbethai, Hodiah, Maaseiah, Kelita, Azariah, Jozabad, Hanan and Pelaiah—instructed the people in the Law while the people were standing there. They read from the Book of the Law of God, making it clear and giving the meaning so that the people could understand what was being read."

There is some difference among scholars as to whether the work of the Levites—not the same ones as those who were on the platform with Ezra—was that of translation or explanation. It might have involved translation since the Law was in Hebrew and the people who had returned from Babylon now spoke Aramaic, a dialect of Hebrew. Without a current, running translation, they might not have been able to understand the text Ezra was reading.[9]

On the other hand, the normal meaning of what the New International Version translates as "making . . . clear" suggests something much closer to what we would call an exposition or sermon. Explanation does not have the same authority as the Word of God itself, but it is important since the Bible is not meant only to be heard and revered but also to be understood, assimilated, and obeyed.

This is the reason for the prominence of sermons in Christian worship and, to speak personally, why I do expository preaching. It is not that other things are not valuable. Liturgical elements of worship can be quite beautiful. Topical sermons can be relevant and moving. But what God has promised to bless and what he has most used to bring blessing is the strict teaching and preaching of his Word. Will the preaching of the Word alone bring revival? Not necessarily, at least not in a mechanical way. Revival is God's work. If we think we can produce it by this or any other mechanical means, we are actually being manipulative, as many Christian orators have tried to be. But although revival does not follow mechanically upon faithful exposition of the Bible, God nevertheless does bless exposition. Characteristically, it is through such Bible preaching that times of renewal and reformation have come.

Here is what one great preacher, Dr. D. Martyn Lloyd-Jones, had to say about the value of preaching:

> What is it that always heralds the dawn of a Reformation or of a Revival? It is renewed preaching. Not only a new interest in preaching but a new kind of preaching. A revival of true preaching has always heralded these great movements in the history of the church. And, of course, when the Reformation and the Revival come they have always led to great and notable periods of the greatest preaching that the church has ever known. As that was true in the beginning as described in the book of Acts, it was also after the Protestant Reformation. Luther, Calvin, Knox, Latimer, Ridley—all these men were great

preachers. In the seventeenth century you had exactly the same thing—the great Puritan preachers and others. And in the eighteenth century, Jonathan Edwards, Whitefield, the Wesleys, Rowlands, and Harris were all great preachers. It was an era of great preaching. Whenever you get Reformation and Revival this is always and inevitably the result.[10]

First, prayer. Second, the public reading of God's Word. Third, the exposition or preaching of it. These were all elements of what was achieved in Nehemiah's day in Jerusalem.

4. Sorrow over sin (v. 9). The result of this anticipatory prayer, the reading of the Law of God, and the explanation of the Law was revival. The first evidence that revival was truly on the way was grief over sin. It was intense grief, though the story does not dwell on it. It says only that "the people had been weeping as they listened to the words of the Law," undoubtedly because they had been convicted by it. This grief must have been intense because Nehemiah, Ezra, and the Levites who were instructing the people had to interrupt the reading and exposition of the Law to deal with it, urging the people to rejoice instead.

"This day is sacred to the LORD your God. Do not mourn or weep," these men told the people (v. 9).

"Go and enjoy choice food and sweet drinks, and send some to those who have nothing prepared. This day is sacred to our Lord. Do not grieve, for the joy of the LORD is your strength," said Nehemiah (v. 10).

"Be still, for this is a sacred day. Do not grieve," said the Levites (v. 11).

Never the Same Again

The people did as they were told, of course. They went away to eat and drink, to provide for others who had little, and "to celebrate with great joy, because they now understood the words that had been made known to them" (v. 12). But they were never the same people again.

Did they sin again? Of course.

Twelve years later, Nehemiah returned to find many sins and a need for renewal. The people of God always need renewal. Still, it was different. These days left a mark on the nation that lasted until and even beyond the time of Jesus Christ.

For one thing, they became a people of God's Book. The events I described took place on the first day of the seventh month. The feast urged on the people by their leaders was that night. But the very next morning, "On the second day of the month, the heads of all the families, along with the priests and the Levites, gathered around Ezra the scribe to give attention to the words of the Law" (v. 13). In other words, Ezra was asked to give *daily* Bible readings (cf. v. 18). Or, as we might say, the heads of the families determined to engage in regular and systematic Bible study.

Second, the life of the people began to revolve around the holy days God had prescribed for worship.

What the remaining verses of the chapter describe is a rediscovery by the people of the instructions for celebrating the Feast of Tabernacles or Booths. It was a harvest festival much like our Thanksgiving, but it was to be done in a way that would remind the people of the days of their wandering in the wilderness. It was a seven-day feast, beginning on the fifteenth of the month. At this point, they still had two weeks to prepare for it. They were to gather sticks and make temporary shelters for themselves outside of or on the roofs of their homes. These would remind them that they were wanderers in the desert for forty years and that God had brought them into the land flowing with milk and honey. When they celebrated the feast, they were to remember that it was God who had provided for them and blessed them abundantly.

Somewhere in this time of preparation, the people must also have observed the Day of Atonement, with its emphasis on sorrow for sin. It came on the tenth of the month. It is not mentioned, probably because the emphasis at this point was so much on gratitude to God and rejoicing.

And why not? In verse 10, Nehemiah had told the people to rejoice: "The joy of the LORD is your strength." It was indeed their strength, for theirs was a happy God, and they were a happy people.

We should be a joyful people too. Indeed, we are frequently told to rejoice. If we do not, it is because we do not love the Word of God as these people did or because we do not obey it.

10

The Sixth Dynamic:
A Nation under God, Part 2

Nehemiah 9:1–37

On the twenty-fourth day of the same month, the Israelites gathered together, fasting and wearing sackcloth and having dust on their heads. Those of Israelite descent had separated themselves from all foreigners. They stood in their places and confessed their sin and the wickedness of their fathers. They stood where they were and read from the Book of the Law of the LORD their God for a quarter of the day, and spent another quarter in confession and in worshiping the LORD their God. . . .

"Now therefore, O our God, the great, mighty and awesome God, who keeps his covenant of love, do not let all this hardship seem trifling in your eyes—the hardship that has come upon us, upon our kings and leaders, upon our priests and prophets, upon our fathers and all your people, from the days of the kings of Assyria until today. In all that has happened to us, you have been just; you have acted faithfully, while we did wrong. Our kings, our leaders, our priests and our fathers did not follow your law; they did not pay attention to your commands or the warnings you gave them. Even while they were in their kingdom, enjoying your great goodness to them in the spacious and fertile land you gave them, they did not serve you or turn from their evil ways. . . .

"We are in great distress."

Nehemiah 9:1–3, 32–35, 37

Several years ago, during the presidency of Jimmy Carter, when the words *born again* had suddenly become common in popular speech, I was often asked in interviews whether America was undergoing a revival. George Gallup Jr., president of the American Institute of Public Opinion, had reported that fifty or sixty million Americans claimed to be born again, and the secular press was discovering that "born again Christians" might be a political force in the nation.

"Is something significant happening?" they asked. "Are we seeing a genuine religious revival?"

Whenever I have been asked that question, my answer has always been no. The reason I say no is quite simple: there is no national consciousness of sin. In fact, there is hardly any *personal* consciousness of sin—very little in the churches and seemingly none at all in the world—and there has never been a revival without this essential element.

Are there fifty million real Christians in America? I do not know; there may be. I think there has been a great deal of effective personal evangelism in our time, particularly among the young who have been influenced by such evangelical student movements as InterVarsity Christian Fellowship, Navigators, and Campus Crusade for Christ. That is good, but it is not the same thing as revival. When revival sweeps over a people, the first evidence is a profound awareness of sin and sorrow for it. This was true of the great Welsh revivals of the last century and of the revivals under the Wesleys the century before that. It was true of the Reformation and of the first revival in recorded history, the revival in Nineveh in response to the preaching of the prophet Jonah.

When revival came to that city, the people declared a fast and donned sackcloth, a sign of mourning. Even the king took part. Then the king issued a decree that said, "Do not let any man or beast, herd or flock, taste anything; do not let them eat or drink. But let man and beast be covered with sackcloth. Let everyone call urgently on God. Let them give up their evil ways and their violence. Who knows? God may yet relent and with compassion turn from his fierce anger so that we will not perish" (Jonah 3:7–9).

The first evidence of a true movement of the Holy Spirit is an awakened conscience, leading to genuine sorrow for sin in God's people. Only after that does revival come.

A Genuine Revival

This is what happened in Jerusalem in Nehemiah's day, and it is why it is proper to speak of this as having been a true revival. There were three parts to this revival, as I pointed out in the last chapter: (1) preaching and hearing the Word of God (chap. 8), (2) sorrow for sin and repentance (chap. 9), and (3) a resulting change of life, formalized by the drafting and signing of a covenant (chap. 10). We have already seen the first element, the prominence given to God's Word. In this chapter, we need to study its profound impact upon the people.

The working of sorrow for sin in the people as a result of the reading and teaching of God's Word was observed in the last chapter, but there it was turned aside or held back by Nehemiah and the Levites. When Ezra read from the Law of Moses, the people must have recognized how far they had fallen from its standards and how guilty they were in the sight of Almighty God. This had affected them even to the point of tears: "The people had been weeping as they listened to the words of the Law" (Neh. 8:9). But that day had been intended as a day of praise and thanksgiving, and for that reason Nehemiah rebuked the tears and sent the people away "to eat and drink, to send portions of food [to those without] and to celebrate with great joy" (v. 12). It was only after this—in fact, it was after the celebration of the Feast of Booths or Tabernacles from the fifteenth to the twenty-second of the month of Tisri—that the special day of penance described in Nehemiah 9 occurred.

I find two very interesting things. First, Nehemiah did not take advantage of the people's first outburst of sorrow to manipulate them and thus push the revival forward. There might have been a temptation to do so. Certainly other religious figures have faced such temptations and have succumbed to them, resorting to tactics of mob psychology to produce apparent spiritual results. Nehemiah apparently felt no need to do this. Rightly so, since if the observed sorrow for sin and repentance was truly from God, it would remain anyway and would not be able to be suppressed. Moreover, the governor wanted to direct the people's thoughts to God and not have them centered on their own feelings, however proper their sorrow and repentance for sin might be. The feast Nehemiah prescribed was a feast of thanksgiving for who God was and for what he had done.

We see the same thing in chapter 9. Here, even after the day of penance is allowed to go forward, the prayer of the Levites, which occupies the bulk of the chapter, is still focused on the greatness of the acts of God.

The second thing I notice is what I have already alluded to: although Nehemiah delayed the day of public repentance by more than three weeks, it did nevertheless occur. It was as strong and genuine then as it would have been at the beginning. This is a way of saying that this movement of repentance was wholly and genuinely of God. If it had been of man only, or if it had been only something that Ezra or Nehemiah had whipped up, it would have faded away.

Genuine Confession and Repentance

The first three verses of chapter 9 tell what finally happened:

On the twenty-fourth day of the same month, the Israelites gathered together, fasting and wearing sackcloth and having dust on their heads. Those of Israelite descent had separated themselves from all foreigners. They stood in their places and confessed their sins and the wickedness of their fathers. They stood where they were and read from the Book of the Law of the LORD their God for a quarter of the day, and spent another quarter in confession and in worshiping the LORD their God.

I also notice two important things about this movement of repentance. First, the confession of the people was once again linked to a reading of God's Law. This had happened on the first day of the month (recorded in chap. 8). It happened again here. It was after the priests had been reading from the "Book of the Law of the LORD their God for a quarter of the day" that the people spent the next quarter of the day (three hours) confessing their sin.

What I am pointing out is more than just an observation. There is a necessary link between the two. Let me explain what I mean by "sin." The *Westminster Shorter Catechism* says, "Sin is any want of conformity unto or transgression of the law of God." That is right: sin is defined by reference to God's Law. This is what makes it sin, as distinguished from an act that is merely mean or offensive or criminal.

Mortimer J. Adler stated it well in his essay on sin in the *Syntopicon* published by the Great Books division of the *Encyclopedia Britannica*:

> The vicious act may be conceived as one which is contrary to nature or reason. The criminal act may be conceived as a violation of the law of man, injurious to the welfare of the state or to its members. Both may involve the notions of responsibility and fault. Both may involve evil and wrongdoing. But unless the act transgresses the law of God, it is not sinful. The divine law which is transgressed may be the natural law that God instills in human reason. But the act is sinful if the person who commits the act turns away from God to the worship or love of other things.[1]

Let me put this definition and the relation of sin to revival in a series of linked statements.

1. There can be no genuine forward moral progress for either a nation or an individual without an acknowledgment of, sorrow for, and a true turning from sin. In other words, nations move forward spiritually and morally only in times of revival.

2. But there can be no true sense of what sin is or a knowledge of why it is sinful without a hearing of and response to the Law of God. That is, we will never acknowledge sin to be sin or grieve over it unless we see it as an offense against God, and the only way we will ever see or sense that it is an offense against God is by seeing our actions as contrary to God's written law.

3. Consequently, revival must be preceded by sound preaching of the whole counsels of God, particularly the Law of God, which we have violated.

The second thing I notice about the people's confession of sin is that it was corporate as well as individualistic. The people not only recognized their own individual sin and confessed it but also understood that they were part of a people or nation and were therefore also collectively guilty. The text expresses this when it says that the people "confessed their sins *and* the wickedness of their fathers" (v. 2, italics added).

It strikes me that this is the exact opposite of what most people do today. When the Jews of Nehemiah's day confessed the sins of their fathers, they acknowledged their guilt for their fathers' sins. Today, if people refer to the sins of their parents at all, it is to excuse themselves rather than to assume any personal share of the responsibility. They blame their wrongdoing on their genes or their upbringing.

> "I know I have a bad temper, but I inherited it from my father. There is nothing I can do about it."
>
> "If you knew the kind of family I was raised in, you would understand why I break my commitments and think of no one but myself."
>
> "Where I come from, everyone steals to get by."

Some forms of psychiatry encourage this kind of thinking. Many church pulpits wallow in it. But when revival comes, people stop trying to excuse themselves by what others, even their parents, have done and instead confess their sin and wrongdoing openly. Like Isaiah, they cry out, "Woe to me! . . . I am ruined! For I am a man of unclean lips, and I live among a people of unclean lips, and my eyes have seen the King, the LORD Almighty" (Isa. 6:5).

The Prayer of the Levites

The main part of Nehemiah 9 consists of a long, formal prayer by the Levites (vv. 5–38), who presumably had been leading the people in the personal expression of sorrow given earlier. This too is a prayer of confession; that is why it is included here. But it is also a prayer that directs the people's thoughts to the goodness and power of God and prepares them for a final appeal to him for mercy in their distressed condition. In structure, it is similar to Psalms 78, 105, and 106, which rehearse the dealings of God with his people, as recorded in the Old Testament history. It is said to be the longest formal prayer in the Old Testament.

The tone of the prayer is set in the opening line, in which the Levites challenge the people to "stand up and praise the LORD your God, who is from everlasting to everlasting" (v. 5). This call inspired James Montgomery to write the hymn that begins:

> Stand up and bless the Lord,
> Ye people of His choice;
> Stand up and bless the Lord your God
> With heart and soul and voice.

Because the prayer praises God, there is something glorious about it, even though it is a prayer of sorrowful confession. John White says it is "stunning in its scope and vision."[2] Derek Kidner writes that in this prayer, "the barely habitable city, the encircling heathen, and the poverty and seeming insignificance of the Jews are all transcended by the glorious reality of God."[3]

The prayer contains three main parts:

1. *The work of God in creation* (vv. 5–6). Since the bulk of the prayer deals with the history of God's dealings with the Jewish people, it is noteworthy that it actually begins by praising God as the Creator of the heavens and earth. This is a good place to begin in and of itself, of course. But the prayer also shows the influence on the people of the Scripture reading of the previous three weeks, since the Old Testament begins with a creation account. In fact, the entire prayer follows an outline based on the content of the early books of the Old Testament.[4]

I sense, as I read the first verses of this prayer, that the Levites of Nehemiah's day were closer to the Scripture and much wiser than most of our contemporary Bible scholars. Today the opening chapters of Genesis are a battleground for competing theories of origins: evolution, theistic evolution, the gap theory, six-day creationism, and progressive creationism. These theories need to be dealt with in their proper place and at a proper time. In fact, I have done so myself in my studies of the early verses of Genesis.[5]

But these theories are not what Genesis 1 and 2 are about. They are about the nature of God, his power and goodness, and about the duty man owes God as his Creator. Nehemiah 9:5–6 reflects this perspective. We cannot escape the irony that although God gives "life to everything, and the multitudes of heaven worship [him]," the masses of mankind do not—not even, it seems, the chosen people.

2. *A review of Israel's history* (vv. 7–31). The second major part of the Levites' prayer is a review of Israel's history.

It begins with God's calling of Abraham (vv. 7–8), as Genesis does. The people must have been thinking about the actual text of Genesis at this time, for Nehemiah 9:7 contains the only Old Testament reference, after Genesis, to the changing of Abraham's name from Abram to Abraham (cf. Gen. 17:5). The name change calls attention to the unilateral way in which God dealt with Abraham, a point made repeatedly throughout this section. Notice that

God is the subject of every action: (1) "*You* . . . chose Abram and brought him out of Ur of the Chaldeans and named him Abraham," (2) "*You* found his heart faithful to you," (3) "*You* made a covenant with him," and (4) "*You* have kept your promise" (italics added). Even the reference to Abraham's faithfulness is framed in this way, for the text does not say, "Abraham was faithful" or "served faithfully" but "*You* [God] found his heart faithful" (v. 8, italics added). The emphasis is entirely upon God. But unlike God, who kept his promises, the people (so it is implied) did not keep theirs. God was utterly faithful; they were not.

The next paragraph recounts the events of the Exodus in brief form (vv. 9–12), and again God is the subject of each action: (1) "*You* saw the suffering of our forefathers in Egypt," (2) "*You* heard their cry at the Red Sea," (3) "*You* sent miraculous signs and wonders against Pharaoh," (4) "*You* knew how arrogantly the Egyptians treated them," (5) "*You* made a name for yourself," (6) "*You* divided the sea before them," (7) "*You* hurled their pursuers into the depths," (8) "By day *you* led them with a pillar of cloud, and by night with a pillar of fire" (italics added). These statements are in narrative form, but in recounting God's acts, the words also reveal God's attributes. They show that he is omniscient ("you saw [our] suffering"), all-powerful ("you sent miraculous signs and wonders against Pharaoh"), righteous ("you hurled their pursuers into the depths"), and merciful, since this is an account of deliverance.

The next paragraph retells the giving of the Mosaic Law at Sinai, the preservation of the people during their passage through the wilderness, and the command to enter and possess the Promised Land (vv. 13–15). In these verses there is an emphasis, as above, on God's sovereign activity: "*You* came down . . . *you* spoke . . . *you* gave them regulations" (italics added), and so on. But the text also stresses the justice of God's commands and God's goodness. These characteristics place the rebellion described in the next verses in a proper light. The people rebelled against God, and it was both wrong (it was against God's righteous commands) and ungrateful (it was against God's goodness).

The verses that come next explicitly describe the rebellion of the people for the first time, and they also contain these two elements. On the one side, the prayer is unstinting in its honest description of the people's rebellious attitude and sin. Their forefathers: (1) "became arrogant" and (2) "stiff-necked," (3) "did not obey [God's] commands," (4) "refused to listen," (5) "failed to remember the miracles," and (6) "appointed a leader in order to return to their slavery" (vv. 16–17). On the other side, God behaved as "a forgiving God, gracious and compassionate, slow to anger and abounding in love" (v. 17). This verse is a direct quotation from Exodus 34:5–7, showing that the people had remembered it also from the earlier reading. (The same verses are quoted in Jonah 4:2.) God was slow to anger even when the people "cast for themselves an image of a calf and said, 'This is your god, who brought you up out of Egypt'" (v. 18).

The same theme continues in the next paragraph (vv. 19–21), which recounts how God sustained the people during their forty years of wilderness wandering.

So also when they eventually entered the Promised Land (vv. 22–25). God drove out many enemies, caused the Israelites to increase in numbers, gave them fortified cities, fertile land, and homes with "wells already dug, vineyards, olive groves and fruit trees." The people "reveled in [God's] great goodness."

Yet they turned from God again. The next three paragraphs (vv. 26–31) describe what became a sad but steady pattern in the nation's life. There was increasing sin and rebellion, followed by God's disciplinary judgments, followed by a temporary return to God, followed by more rebellion, sin, and apostasy. The list of Israel's sins grows very specific in these paragraphs, as all true confession of sin must: (1) "they were disobedient and rebelled," (2) "they put your law behind their backs," (3) "they killed your prophets," (4) "they committed awful blasphemies," (5) "they again did what was evil in your sight," (6) "they became arrogant and disobeyed your commands," (7) "they sinned against your ordinances," (8) "stubbornly they turned their backs on you, became stiff-necked and refused to listen," (9) "they paid no attention." Yet alongside this swelling cacophony of rebellious voices, God continued to speak quietly and show mercy. The last line says, "But in your great mercy you did not put an end to them or abandon them, for you are a gracious and merciful God" (v. 31).

3. An appeal for God's mercy in the present distress (vv. 32–37). As the litany of the people's sins has built to a climax, so have the repeated affirmations of God's patience, goodness, and mercy. It is to these blessed characteristics of God that the final section of the prayer now makes eloquent appeal:

> Now therefore, O our God, the great, mighty and awesome God, who keeps his covenant of love, do not let all this hardship seem trifling in your eyes—the hardship that has come upon us, upon our kings and leaders, upon our priests and prophets, upon our fathers and all your people, from the days of the kings of Assyria until today. In all that has happened to us, you have been just; you have acted faithfully, while we did wrong. Our kings, our leaders, our priests and our fathers did not follow your law; they did not pay attention to your commands or the warnings you gave them. Even while they were in their kingdom, enjoying your great goodness to them in the spacious and fertile land you gave them, they did not serve you or turn from their evil ways.
>
> But see, we are slaves today, slaves in the land you gave our forefathers so they could eat its fruit and the other good things it produces. Because of our sins, its abundant harvest goes to the kings you have placed over us. They rule our bodies and our cattle as they please. We are in great distress.

Do you feel the need to confess your sin to God? If so, that is how to do it—completely and forthrightly! The prayer of the Levites in Jerusalem in the days of Nehemiah is a model confession. It shows how to find spiritual blessing again.

"If My People"

What do we need to do? The answer is no mystery. It is clearly stated in 2 Chronicles 7:14: "If my people, who are called by my name, will humble themselves and pray and seek my face and turn from their wicked ways, then will I hear from heaven and will forgive their sin and will heal their land." These are the steps to God's blessing.

1. *We must humble ourselves.* By nature we are not humble. It is only when we come before God that we are genuinely humbled, for it is then that we see ourselves as the sinful and rebellious creatures we really are.

2. *We must pray.* We do not naturally pray. Why? Because we believe we are self-sufficient. This is why God often has to bring us very low. It is often only in the depths of life, when everything is crumbling around us, that we are willing to turn from ourselves to God and ask him for the help we need.

3. *We must seek God's face.* To seek God's face means to seek his favor rather than the favor of the world around us and to seek his will rather than our own. To seek God's face means a radical change in the use of our time, talents, resources, and lifestyle.

4. *We must turn from our wicked ways.* If we do not think we have wicked ways, we will not turn from them—and we are fooling ourselves. When God brings the reality of our sin home to us, we will find ourselves distressed by sin and unwilling to rest until we confess it to God, find his forgiveness, and turn from everything that is displeasing to him. *Everything!* Not just the "great" sins. Not just the sins that have obviously gotten us into trouble or that offend others. All sins. God does not ask for 50 percent of what we are or look only for 60 percent righteousness. He wants all of us, and he insists on genuine holiness. We cannot serve God and sin too.

Is it difficult to repent? It certainly is! Nothing is harder or goes more against the grain of our sinful natures, but it is necessary for personal happiness and God's blessing. The promise is that if we will repent of our sins, then God will hear from heaven (he never turns a deaf ear to the repentant), forgive our sin (how much we need it), and heal our land.

11

The Sixth Dynamic:
A Nation under God, Part 3

Nehemiah 9:38–10:39

In view of all this, we are making a binding agreement, putting it in writing, and our leaders, our Levites and our priests are affixing their seals to it.

. . . all these now join their brothers the nobles, and bind themselves with a curse and an oath to follow the Law of God given through Moses the servant of God and to obey carefully all the commands, regulations and decrees of the LORD our Lord.

We promise not to give our daughters in marriage to the peoples around us or take their daughters for our sons.

When the neighboring peoples bring merchandise or grain to sell on the Sabbath, we will not buy from them on the Sabbath or on any holy day. Every seventh year we will forgo working the land and will cancel all debts.

We assume the responsibility for carrying out the commands to give a third of a shekel each year for the service of the house of our God. . . .

We also assume responsibility for bringing to the house of the LORD each year the firstfruits of our crops and of every fruit tree.

As it is also written in the Law, we will bring the firstborn of our sons and of our cattle, of our herds and of our flocks to the house of our God, to the priests ministering there.

Moreover, we will bring to the storerooms of the house of our God, to the priests, the first of our ground meal, of our grain offerings, of the fruit of all our trees and of our new wine and oil. And we will bring a tithe of our crops to the Levites. . . .

We will not neglect the house of our God.

Nehemiah 9:38; 10:29–32, 35–37, 39

We live in a day of psychiatry and psychology. Thousands of people visit their counselors on a weekly or biweekly basis. Yet one thing that has always puzzled me is why there is so little change in most of these people's lives, why their problems persist so long, and why their therapy frequently continues for years. I once asked a psychologist friend, "Why is there so little change through therapy?"

My friend replied, "It is because people really do not want to change. No changes ever take place unless you want them."

I have thought about that since and am convinced that it applies to spiritual change too. Many people "talk the talk," but they do not show growth in their walks with Jesus Christ because they do not want to change the way they are living. They do not want to give up their sins or reorder their priorities. They know they should. At times they might even be moved to tears by their failures. But they do not surge ahead because basically they want to do exactly as they have been doing.

There must be commitment to something different or bigger or grander than ourselves if we are to make progress in our lives.

Three Steps to Revival

Things changed radically in Jerusalem under the governorship of Nehemiah and the pastoring of Ezra. I have been calling it a revival, because that is what it was. Revival means coming to spiritual life again. The people had been spiritually dead. Now they revived, and the changes that came transformed their nation and culture permanently. Some of these changes lasted more than four hundred years, until and even beyond the time of Jesus Christ.

What were the steps of this revival? We have already seen two of them. The first stage was the reading, teaching, and hearing of the Word of God. It was led by Ezra the priest, who was the spiritual head of the nation. Ezra called an assembly on the first day of the month of Tisri, at which he read from the Law from six in the morning until noon. One group of thirteen Levites accompanied him, probably assisting with the long reading, while another group of thirteen Levites circulated among the people to explain the words of the Law and apply them. The result of this was a twofold awakening of the people. They were awakened to their sin, which they showed by weeping. They also were awakened to the wonders of the Law. They showed this by their continuing attention to the Word of God.

Beginning with the second day of the month of Tisri, the heads of the families attended daily readings of the Law. We would call these daily Bible studies. Then, on the twenty-fourth day of the month, there was a second solemn assembly at which the people confessed their sins together.

This was the second stage of the revival. On this day, following another reading of the Law, the people spent three hours in formal confession. Then the Levites led them in a formal prayer of confession, the longest recorded prayer in the Old Testament. The prayer is distinguished by a recitation of God's sovereign acts and mercies toward the people during the years of their national history, a forthright confession of the people's stiff-necked rebellion and persistent idolatries, and a plea for God's mercy to them in their distress.

Ah, but many people have expressed sorrow for sin and acknowledged their distress without changing. That is why the third stage of this revival, recounted for us in Nehemiah 10, is so critical. The third stage is a formal commitment to change, expressed in a covenant. The text refers to it as "a binding agreement" (Neh. 9:38) to which the leaders, Levites, and priests formally affixed their seals, the equivalent of a signature.

Four different categories of people signed the document.

At the head of the list of signatories are Nehemiah and Zedekiah (v. 1). In the New International Version, Zedekiah seems to belong to the list of priests in verses 2–8. But in the Hebrew, Nehemiah and Zedekiah are joined by the conjunction *and*, which seems to set the two of them apart as a special group representing the civil power. Probably Zedekiah was Nehemiah's chief secretary. James B. Pritchard indicates that legal documents were normally attested by a scribe and witnesses and that a high official's secretary often signed with him in second place.[1]

The second category of signatories contains the names of Israel's priests (vv. 2–8). There are twenty-one names in this list, the majority of which (at least fifteen) are family names. We can tell this by comparing these verses with chapter 12, verses 12–21, where the names of the priestly families are given explicitly. Ezra belonged to the family of Seraiah (cf. Ezra 7:1), the name that heads the list, which most scholars feel explains why Ezra's name does not appear separately.

The third category contains seventeen names of Levites (vv. 9–13). Some of these are family names, but most are individuals, a number of whom appear in the list of Levites who explained and applied the Law on the day it was first read, according to Nehemiah 8:7. Hashabiah was one of the builders of the wall (Neh. 3:17).

The final category contains the names of forty-four of the noble families of Israel (vv. 14–27). Many of these names correspond to the names of the families that are said to have returned with the first group of exiles, according to Ezra 2 and Nehemiah 7. Some of the names also appear among the list of wall builders in Nehemiah 3.

These signers of the covenant were meant to represent the entire people, as the concluding postscript to the list of names (vv. 28–29) clearly indicates:

> The rest of the people—priests, Levites, gatekeepers, singers, temple servants and all who separated themselves from the neighboring peoples for the sake of the Law of God, together with their wives and all their sons and daughters who are able to understand—all these now join their brothers the nobles, and bind themselves with a curse and an oath to follow the Law of God given through Moses the servant of God and to obey carefully all the commands, regulations and decrees of the LORD our Lord.

It is hard to imagine a more formal agreement on the part of the people, or a more intense commitment to forward spiritual change.

Characteristics of the Covenant

Change for the sake of mere change means nothing, of course. What matters is the direction of the change. So, before we examine the specifics of the covenant, it will be helpful to see its three characteristics, which indicate where the people saw themselves heading.

1. The authority of the Bible. Everything in this formal commitment by the people is in response to what they understood to be the demands of the Old Testament Law. We see this in the promises made; each is in response to a specific Old Testament demand, most repeated in several settings throughout the Pentateuch. Again, the covenant also begins with two explicit references to the Law, one in verse 28 and one in verse 29. Verse 28 defines the signers of the covenant as those who had "separated themselves from the neighboring peoples *for the sake of the Law of God*" (italics added). Verse 29 tells how these same people bound themselves "with a curse and an oath *to follow the Law of God given through Moses the servant of God* and to obey carefully all the commands, regulations and decrees of the LORD our Lord" (italics added).

This means that the people were responding to the authority of Scripture. There are other kinds of commitment, of course: commitment to a cause, to the demands of legal contract, to a person. But no level of commitment is higher or of greater importance than this, for the simple reason that nothing deserves a higher level of service or obedience from us than God, and God has expressed his will in Scripture.

This is what the so-called battle for the Bible in our day is all about. Some have ridiculed it as a crusade by ignorant, insecure people who think the universe is shaken whenever a detail of the Bible is challenged, but that is not it at all. The issue is whether the Bible is God's Book, rather than man's, and whether God is going to be acknowledged as the sovereign Lord he is. If God is God, and if God has spoken to us in the Bible, as the church has always confessed he has, then this Book is supreme over us. We must be bound by it, and this means we must order our lives accordingly. If the Bible says, "You shall not steal" (Exod. 20:15), then we must not steal—not because we are likely to get in trouble and possibly even go to jail if we do but because God has told us not to. If the Bible says, "You shall not commit adultery" (Exod. 20:14), then we must not commit adultery. It is the same for all the Bible's commands, admonitions, and principles.

The impressive thing about the covenant in Nehemiah 9 is that the people were concerned to do this. It shows they were truly converted and they wanted to go forward in their spiritual relationship.

2. The importance of the temple. Although the specific promises of verses 30–39 cover a wide spectrum of these ancient Jews' lives, a surprising portion deal with the temple and the temple worship: the temple tax, the firstfruits of the crops and trees, the regular offerings, and the tithe. The construction of the temple had been a first concern of the returning exiles years before. Their slowness in building it had been a burden of the minor prophet Haggai. Continuing provision for the temple concerned Ezra.

We might think that Nehemiah, the civil ruler, would not have been concerned for the temple since his efforts had been so strongly directed to rebuilding the city's wall. But now we learn differently. Nehemiah was committed to the temple too. Why? Because he knew the temple and the worship of God that went on there would bind the people into a self-conscious and cohesive nation. As Howard F. Vos says, "The temple . . . provided the religious and social cement to bind members of the community to each other, and preeminently to God and his service."[2] This cohesion would be difficult to maintain. At the very end of the book of Nehemiah as well as in the book of the minor prophet Malachi, we find that later generations of Jews quite easily neglected their tithes and allowed the temple services to languish.

3. The responsibility of the people. The third striking characteristic of this covenant is the people's strong sense of responsibility. Nothing in the covenant looks to other people to do what they should do. Nothing sets some of them apart from these responsibilities, or assigns specific tasks to one group and other tasks to another. The dominant word is *we*, referring to the whole people together. It was as one whole people that they took it upon themselves to keep God's entire law.

Who else would do it?

It is the same for us in our response as Christians to the teachings of Jesus Christ. If we will not obey him, live holy lives, and be his witnesses in this world, it is certain that no one else will. The responsibility is ours alone.

Six Essential Commitments

The people had obligated themselves to keep the whole Law, according to verses 28 and 29. But a general promise without specifics does not mean much. Therefore, the people expressed their intentions in a series of specific commitments. Their choice showed clearly it was these items that needed their attention.

1. The family (v. 30). Wisely they began with the family, promising not to intermarry with the peoples of the lands roundabout. This was not racial snobbery or prejudice, since the Jewish people had always contained some individuals of other races. Moses had married an Ethiopian. Rahab of Jericho and Ruth the Moabitess had readily been included within Israel. The concern was not racial but religious, as the key verses in Exodus 34:12–16 make clear. It was the danger of having the people be led away to the worship of the pagan gods of the surrounding nations as a result of intermarriages. Ezra had dealt with the problem thirteen years earlier. Malachi spoke against it. Even Nehemiah would have to face it again at the very end of his period of service (chap. 13).

There is a reason the defense of godly families comes first in this list of concerns: the family is the basic unit of society, godly or otherwise. In fact, all great social institutions have come from it. The home was the original seat of education, the first school. So grammar and high schools, colleges, universities, and other kinds of training centers owe their existence to this basic family function. The home was the first hospital. Indeed, for centuries it was the only place for the care of the sick and dying. All medical facilities owe their existence to the home. So also with government. Patriarchal societies, monarchies, and democracies have developed from the home. The significance of this is that if the family stands, society will stand. But if the family is destroyed, the nation will deteriorate rapidly.

It works the other way too. When a culture goes into moral decline, the family structure grows weak.

This is why Communist and other revolutionary governments have been so anxious to weaken or destroy the family, setting children against parents and sometimes physically separating children, husbands, and wives. They know that the family is a strong unit of its own and that if they can destroy it, they will have greater success in building a correspondingly strong allegiance to the state. It is also why Christians must defend the family, in spite of many contemporary attempts to tear it down. We must do it for the good of our country and for Christianity itself.

The apostle Paul knew this. In words that echo the concern of the Jewish people under Nehemiah, he wrote, "Do not be yoked together with unbelievers. For what do righteousness and wickedness have in common? Or what fellowship can light have with darkness? . . . What does a believer have in common with an unbeliever? . . . Dear friends, let us purify ourselves from everything that contaminates body and spirit, perfecting holiness out of reverence for God" (2 Cor. 6:14–15; 7:1).

2. *The Sabbath* (v. 31). The second specific commitment of the people on this great covenant day was to keep the Sabbath by abstaining from all commercial activity and to observe the seventh-year Sabbath of the land, in which the fields would not be worked. The requirement has precedent in God's resting from creation on the seventh day and goes back to the Ten Commandments, which say, "Remember the Sabbath day by keeping it holy" (Exod. 20:8).

In my opinion, Christians are not under the specific Sabbath laws of the Old Testament. We have been delivered from keeping "special days and months and seasons and years" (Gal. 4:10). But that is not the whole story. True, we have not been commanded to observe an inactive Sabbath. But we have been given a new day, the Lord's Day, to enjoy. Our day is not a sober day of withdrawal. It is a day of active, joyful worship. But do we actually enjoy it as such? Do we use it for worship, Christian service, and witness? Or do we only pretend to do it, spending a few formal moments in church in order to be free to spend the rest of the day watching football or merely lounging around?

Why don't you make a commitment to make Sunday a day when you focus on Christian concerns specifically? I have a friend in the ministry who tells his people, "If you want to grow in the Christian life, determine to come to church more than once a week, witness to your friends, ask your pastor for a job, and then get busy serving Jesus." It is not a bad formula.

3. *The temple tax* (vv. 32–33). The third matter in which the people of Jerusalem made a formal commitment was the paying of the temple tax. Here we have two problems. The first is technical. In the Pentateuch, according to Exodus 30:11–16, the temple tax had been fixed at half a shekel, while here, in Nehemiah 10:32, it is a third of a shekel. Since not even the priests were free to alter God's Law, some explanation is in order. Usually this is explained by assuming that the Jerusalem and Babylonian shekels had different valuations, which is not unlikely, or by noting that in Exodus the tax was to be paid only when a census was taken, while in Nehemiah it was to be paid annually.

The bigger problem is in relating this temple tax to ourselves. We do not have anything like a large central temple in our religious systems, and the more general matter of support of Christian work by our stewardship is covered later in reference to the tithe (see number 6 below). Is the matter of the temple tax therefore completely irrelevant to us?

I do not think so. Rather, I think that this item (as well as the added concern to provide wood and other necessary supplies for the temple, which comes next) shows a priority for having a central location for corporate worship and for God's service. Let me put it this way: having a fixed place where the people could meet together and worship God mattered to them. Suppose we had been there and could have said, "But what does it matter whether or not you have the temple? Can't you each worship God privately or in your homes?" The people would have replied that of course they could worship God privately, and did. Nevertheless, it mattered that they could come together as one people and give visible demonstration of their common beliefs and experience.

We need similar focal points for Christian faith today. The obvious ones are the local churches.

I notice here that although the Persian kings had made certain important provisions for the Jewish temple (cf. Ezra 6:8–10), the people did not expect them to keep on doing that but rather assumed responsibility for providing for the temple services themselves. That is also a Christian responsibility. The government may provide certain advantages to churches and other "charitable" organizations, but we cannot expect government to support them. Nor should it. If Christians do not support the Lord's work, the Lord's work will not be supported.

4. *Additional provisions for the temple* (vv. 34–35). The people of Jerusalem seem not to have been content merely with paying the temple tax. They recognized that the temple service required other things that they also could provide, specifically wood for the great altar and the firstfruits of their crops and trees. They promised to supply them. In the same way, there are things we can give to Christian work aside from money. Service organizations need donations of food and clothing. We can offer our expertise in certain areas. Most important, we can contribute time.

5. *Dedication of the firstborn* (v. 36). The Law declared that the firstborn of every household, as well as the firstborn of all the flocks, belonged to the Lord. In practice, the people generally redeemed the firstborn by payment of a redemption price, but the practice reminded them that all life is a gift from God and is owed to him. Our lives also belong to God, first because of creation (he made us) and second because of redemption (God bought us for himself by the blood of Christ). This is why Paul said, "For to me, to live is Christ and to die is gain" (Phil. 1:21) and "I have been crucified with Christ and I no longer live, but Christ lives in me" (Gal. 2:20).

6. *The tithe* (vv. 37–39). I feel about the tithe much the way I feel about the Sabbath, having said often that I see no specific passage in the New Testament that lays the tithe upon Christians as legal obligation. But as I said before, that is not the whole story. It is true that Christians are not under the specifics of the Old Testament legislation, but where ethical issues are concerned, it is always the case that when you pass from the Old Testament to the New, the standard goes up rather than down. The Old Testament Jew was to give a straight 10 percent of his income to the Lord. It was a simple matter in order

to avoid any manipulation of the angles, prevarication, or confusion. It was 10 percent of everything he received: wages, tips, gifts, an inheritance, a lottery! And it was for everybody: the young, the old, wives, husbands, students, the rich, the poor. It was the minimum. That much was owed to the Lord. The Jew was to "pay" the tithe. After that, if he had been particularly blessed and wanted to, he could give additional gifts and offerings.

What is our principle today? It is higher, as I indicated. It is not 10 percent but 100 percent. All we are and have is the Lord's. Our question is not how much we are required to give but rather how much it is proper to keep for ourselves for our maintenance.

Jesus stated the principle in the Sermon on the Mount:

> Do not store up for yourselves treasures on earth, where moth and rust destroy, and where thieves break in and steal. But store up for yourselves treasures in heaven, where moth and rust do not destroy, and where thieves do not break in and steal. For where your treasure is, there your heart will be also. . . . No one can serve two masters. . . . You cannot serve both God and money.
>
> Matthew 6:19–21, 24

I call this "lifestyle stewardship," a pattern of life in which we have first given ourselves to the Lord and then regularly give ourselves to others in his name (cf. 2 Cor. 8:5).

Covenants Today

The Christian church is of a divided mind about covenants. On the one hand, there are those who distrust them, primarily because they rightly distrust any human ability to keep covenants. "Whenever you promise God that you will do something, you are sure to break that promise," they argue. That is generally true, of course. At the very least, the reservations of these people warn us that none of us should subscribe to a covenant or covenants lightly.

On the other hand, it is impossible to write off all formal commitments. The very act of becoming a Christian is something of a covenant, for when we repent of our sin and turn in faith to Christ as our Savior, we also promise to follow him and serve him as our Lord. When we are baptized we enter into a covenant. When we join a church we make a covenant. In our church the promise is "to make diligent use of the means of grace, to share faithfully in the worship and service of the church, to give of your substance as the Lord may prosper you, and to give your whole heart to the service of Christ and his kingdom throughout the world." Why should other important spiritual steps be any different? Why should we not frequently determine to change for the better—and covenant to do so?

I suggest that you formally covenant to put God first in everything you do: order your marriage or family according to the Bible's standards, set aside one day in seven to worship and serve God in the company of other Christians, tithe your income for the Lord's work—and do whatever else God puts it upon your mind to do for him. And make it a lifetime commitment!

12

The Seventh Dynamic:
Urban Renewal

Nehemiah 11:1–12:26

Now the leaders of the people settled in Jerusalem, and the rest of the people cast lots to bring one out of every ten to live in Jerusalem, the holy city, while the remaining nine were to stay in their own towns. The people commended all the men who volunteered to live in Jerusalem.

These are the provincial leaders who settled in Jerusalem (now some Israelites, priests, Levites, temple servants and descendants of Solomon's servants lived in the towns of Judah, each on his own property in the various towns, while other people from both Judah and Benjamin lived in Jerusalem):

From the descendants of Judah. . . .

From the descendants of Benjamin. . . .

From the priests. . . .

From the Levites. . . .

The gatekeepers. . . .

These were the priests and Levites who returned with Zerubbabel son of Shealtiel and with Jeshua. . . .

These were the leaders of the priests and their associates. . . .

These were the heads of the priestly families. . . .

Mattaniah, Bakbukiah, Obadiah, Meshullam, Talmon and Akkub were gatekeep-
ers who guarded the storerooms at the gates. They served in the days of Joiakim son of
Jeshua, the son of Jozadak, and in the days of Nehemiah the governor and of Ezra the
priest and scribe.

Nehemiah 11:1–4, 7, 10, 15, 19; 12:1, 7, 12, 25–26

I do not need to prove the accelerating urbanization of the world in this century. At the time of Jesus Christ, there were only about 250 million people in the world, about equal to the current population of the United States. It took fifteen hundred years for that to double to 0.5 billion, at the time of the Protestant Reformation. It doubled again by the end of the eighteenth century, to 1 billion in three hundred years. By the start of the twentieth century, one hundred years later, it was 2 billion. Today there are 5.1 billion people in the world. By the end of the twentieth century, the population of the world is expected to reach 6 billion. *The vast majority of these new people will live in cities.*

Two hundred years ago, only 2.5 percent of the world's population lived in cities. The figure was 40 percent by 1970. Today it is almost half, and it is projected to reach a startling 90 percent by the year 2000.

How many of the world's cities do you suppose have more than a million inhabitants? The answer to that question is 175. Twenty-nine of these are in the United States, but the United States does not have the largest number of these megacities. China and Russia have more cities with more than a million persons than all other countries. The fastest-growing cities in the world are in Latin America. Mexico City, now the largest city in the world, has 20 million residents. By the year 2000, India will have twenty cities with 20 million residents. In America, 70 percent of the citizens now live in urban areas.

What does that say about the proper focus for Christian witness today? What does it suggest for our mission priorities?

Jerusalem in the Time of Nehemiah

Our situation is different from the one that confronted Nehemiah. We have cities that are overflowing. He had a city that was nearly empty. Nevertheless, there are surprising similarities. Nehemiah wanted to populate Jerusalem. We need to populate our largely secular cities with Christians in order to reach this vast urban majority for Jesus Christ.

The similarities go beyond that, particularly when we consider the difficulties Nehemiah faced in reoccupying the city. The problem is outlined briefly in Nehemiah 7:4: "Now the city was large and spacious, but there were few people in it, and the houses had not yet been rebuilt." Why had the city not been occupied? There were a number of reasons. For one thing, it had been without a wall for 142 years.[1] This meant that the city had been defenseless for that time, and as a result it was dangerous to live there. In case of an invasion, a family living in the country could run away and hide, perhaps only losing their cattle and crops. But a person in the city was stuck. He was easy to attack, and the city, because it had few people, had few defenders.

Again, in Nehemiah's day Jerusalem was an example of what we call urban blight. The city had been ravaged by invading armies, stripped of anything valuable more quickly and completely than an abandoned car in the ghetto. The houses as well as the walls were destroyed. Jerusalem was filled with rubble. And then, during the century and a half of its nonoccupation, grass and trees would have grown up in the yards, streets, and passageways. It was a difficult place to live. It was an even more difficult place to make a living.

What did Nehemiah do? The eleventh chapter tells about it. First, no doubt at Nehemiah's urging, the leaders moved to the newly walled city. Then the people cast lots to select one out of every ten Israelites to join them.

Just like that!

Because it was important that the city be occupied!

I suggest that something exactly like that needs to be done by Christian people today. For too long we have been guilty of what has been called "white flight" from the cities. We have moved away from the action, where we have been needed, to where it is nice! And because of our suburban, rural orientation, we have carried the same pattern over into our approach to world missions. We have focused on the remotest areas, while the people in those areas have been leaving them and streaming into metropolitan environments. The greatest challenge to Christian witness today is to establish an evangelical presence in the world's cities.

Ronald J. Sider, associate professor of theology at Eastern Baptist Theological Seminary in Philadelphia, puts it in stark terms: "Evangelicals must reverse the continuing evangelical flight from the cities. . . . Tens of thousands of evangelicals ought to move back into the city. . . . If one percent of evangelicals living outside the inner city had the faith and courage to move in town, evangelicals would fundamentally alter the history of urban America."[2]

Anatomy of a Plan

At first glance, the list of names and places in Nehemiah 11 seems even more tedious and uninteresting than the earlier lists in chapters 3, 7, and 10. But the list actually reflects a great strategy. It highlights several parts of Nehemiah's plan.

1. Repopulation. The first and most obvious step in the renewal of Jerusalem was the city's repopulation. The list of people in chapter 11 begins with the families of two tribes: Judah and Benjamin. This is appropriate since Jerusalem was in the tribal territory of Judah and bordered Benjamin, which extended northward from it. Moreover, most of the people were from those tribes. They had been the chief tribes of the southern kingdom of Judah and were therefore the last to have been overthrown. Samaria, the capital of the northern kingdom of Israel, had been overthrown in 721 BC. Jerusalem fell in 586 BC. The text mentions two families of Judah (vv. 4–6) and three families of Benjamin (vv. 7–9).

After this there are lists of priests, Levites, gatekeepers, temple servants, and a variety of city officers (vv. 10–24), followed by a list of cities outside Jerusalem where many of the people settled. Chapter 12 gives the ancestry of these leaders and families, going back to those who originally had come to Jerusalem under Zerubbabel (12:1–26).

We can do some interesting calculations on the basis of the numbers provided. If the numbers of those said to have settled in Jerusalem are added up, the total of adult males comes to 3,044. If we add women and children to that, the resulting population of Jerusalem at this time was probably about 10,000, conservatively estimated. Since this was intended to be one-tenth of the entire population, the total number of Jews in Judah would have been about 100,000.[3]

2. Organization. The second striking thing about this chapter is the obvious organization of the people. Certainly it is one thing Nehemiah intended to make clear when he composed it. This was no rabble of refugees merely settling down anywhere. These people knew their ancestry and their present family and religious leaders. Jerusalem had a government. Even the Jews who settled outside the city did not settle just anywhere. The lists at the end of chapter 11 suggest that they tried to settle in their ancestral homes.

The first leader mentioned is Joel son of Zicri. He was the "chief officer" of the descendants of Benjamin.

The next officer mentioned is Judah son of Hassenuah. The Hebrew describes him as being "second in command of the city." This has created a problem for most commentators since, in Nehemiah 7:2, Hanani is said to have been "put in charge" of the city and Hannaniah is said to have been made the "commander of the citadel"; that is, they occupied positions one and two. One way of resolving the difficulty is to translate the words describing Judah's responsibility as "over the Second District of the city," as the New International Version and some other versions do. But it is equally possible (better, in my opinion) to see the structure as follows:

Nehemiah, governor of the province of Judah
Hanani, civil ruler (first in command) of Jerusalem

Hannaniah, military commander (first in command) of Jerusalem
Judah of Benjamin, second in command of the city (probably under Hanani)

Joel would have represented the concerns of the descendants of Benjamin, and presumably there would have been an officer to represent Judah even though, for some reason, he is not mentioned here.

In the following verses, we are given the name of the chief officer of the priests: Zabdiel son of Haggedolim.

The Levites are likewise organized. Shabbethai and Jozabad were two of their officers. Mattaniah was the director who led in thanksgiving and prayer. Bakbukiah was second under him. Another responsible Levite was Abda son of Shammua.

Akkub and Talmon were the heads of the gatekeepers.

Ziha and Gishpa were in charge of the temple servants.

Verse 22 tells us that the chief officer of the Levites in Jerusalem was Uzzi son of Bani.

Verse 24 adds that Pethahiah "was the king's agent in all affairs relating to the people." Some of these leaders are mentioned again in chapter 12 (Mattaniah, vv. 8, 25; Bakbukiah, vv. 9, 25; Uzzi, v. 19;[4] Talmon, v. 25; Akkub, v. 25).

3. Participation. The third characteristic of this resettlement was the active participation of the people in what was going on. It may be a bit excessive to call this democracy, but it was not arbitrary action by Nehemiah either. Earlier, in chapter 7, Nehemiah did exercise his prerogative as governor by appointing Hanani as the chief civil officer of Jerusalem and Hananiah as the military commander. But we do not have any suggestion of that here. The implication seems to be that each of the tribes and religious groupings selected its own leaders.

Another indication of the participatory spirit that prevailed is the reference in verse 2 to those who "volunteered" to live in Jerusalem. It is hard to tell what this refers to. It seems to refer to those who were chosen by lot, according to verse 1, although this would be a strange thing to say in such circumstances. If it does refer to these people, it would mean that although they were chosen by lot, they nevertheless relocated to the city willingly. On the other hand, it could refer to others who volunteered to accompany them. In either case, the picture is of an arrangement upon which the people as a whole agreed. It was not a case of forcible uprooting and migration. Rather, the people wanted the city to prosper and so willingly moved there.

4. A religious base. The fourth characteristic of Nehemiah's effort to revitalize Jerusalem was that he had a religious base. The chapter begins with an account of how one in ten Jewish laypersons was chosen to relocate, but little is said about them. The bulk of the chapter (and the next chapter) details the families of priests, Levites, and other religious leaders who settled in the city.

Why? Obviously because Nehemiah knew, as we also should know, that a community holds together only by some higher allegiance or priority and that the only truly adequate base for real brotherhood or community among people is devotion to God. Without this, the people soon become little more than competing or warring factions. Cyril Barber says it well:

> A strong religious commitment is essential if a democratic form of administration is to succeed. Without adequate spiritual values it is hard, if not impossible, to retain the idea of obligation and responsibility. Individualism cannot long be held in check by the concept of a calling embodying good works and self-restraint. When this control is weakened, legislation takes the place of spiritual convictions and becomes the foundation of the community. And with the increase in legislation there is a corresponding increase in bureaucracy with a minimizing of efficiency and a diminution of personal worth.[5]

Jerusalem had a religious base. Therefore, there was cohesion and efficiency among the people, as well as a strong sense of personal worth.

Impacting Our Cities

But enough of Nehemiah's plan. I said at the beginning that we also must populate our cities in a Christian manner. How shall *we* do this? What should be *our* plan? I suggest that what we need to establish in our cities are models of Christian community. This goal should have the following essential elements:

1. We must live in the cities. Not every Christian needs to live in our cities, but far more should live in them than do. How many? It is hard to say. In Nehemiah's day, in which the economy was largely agricultural, the figure was one in ten—plus others who lived in the cities roundabout. In America in our day, where the economy is industrial and service based rather than agricultural, 50 percent of the general population live in cities. That suggests that at least 50 percent of the Christian population should also. But since this percentage is going up, and since we want to be ahead of the times rather than lagging behind, we should probably lead the way, with an even higher percentage of evangelicals relocating to the urban areas.

Our goal should be a Christian presence in each block of each major city. My model for this is the example of E. V. Hill, pastor of the Mount Zion Missionary Baptist Church of Los Angeles. Hill is one of the great urban leaders of our time. Before he entered the Christian ministry, he lived in Texas, where he was a ward leader for the Democratic party. His assignment was to get out the vote for Democratic candidates, and his chief strategy for doing this was to have a block captain for each block of his ward. On election days, the block captains were to contact all residents of their blocks to make sure they voted. When Hill came to Los Angeles, he asked himself why he should not do that for the kingdom of God, if he had done it for the Democrats. Why not have a Christian block captain for every block of Los Angeles?

Does that sound crazy? Impossible?

It is not so absurd as you might think. How many blocks do you suppose are in the city of Los Angeles? The answer: about 9,000. In E. V. Hill's area of the city, south central Los Angeles, the number is 3,100. That is what Dr. Hill's church tackled. By the time I first heard him tell about this goal, the church had already established a Christian presence in 1,900 blocks of the area.

How many blocks do we have in the immediate area of Tenth Presbyterian Church in Philadelphia, the church I serve? The area is bounded by Market Street on the north and South Street on the south. Starting at Broad Street, which divides Center City in two, and going westward toward the Schuylkill River, the area in which Tenth Church is located, there are 74 blocks. Just 74! And if the area is extended eastward toward the Delaware River, taking in the entire Center City residential area east to west, there are only 87 blocks more. Only 161 blocks in Center City! It should not be too difficult to have a multiple Christian presence in each block of that small area. There should be a weekly Bible study in each block.

The same magnitude of statistics should prevail for the residential areas of most other U.S. cities.

Would such an effort be felt? It would.

Hill tells of what happened in Los Angeles on one occasion. One man had been so put off by the captain of the block in which he lived—she was always inviting him to church and other religious meetings—that he decided to move all the way across Los Angeles. The truck came. He loaded up his possessions. His block captain came out to say good-bye. The truck started off. But as soon as he was gone, his block captain went back into the house, got out the directory of Mount Zion block captains in Los Angeles, and found the person in charge of the block to which her offended neighbor was moving. When he arrived at his new home, there was his new block captain standing on the street to welcome him and invite him to church.

His comment was a classic. He said, "My God, they're everywhere." That should be our goal—to have a visible presence everywhere in the cities.

2. We must be a community in the cities. It is not enough just to be in the cities, of course. We must also be together in the cities; we must be a Christian community. It is only as a community that we can model what we are recommending. I think of the lines of the great twentieth-century poet T. S. Eliot:

When the Stranger says: "What is the meaning of this city?
Do you huddle close together because you love each other?"
What will you answer? "We all dwell together
To make money from each other"? or "This is a community"?

Chorus from "The Rock"

Anthony T. Evans is a successful black pastor in Dallas, Texas. He is an excellent Bible expositor, and his ministry goal is to have the population centers of America experience spiritual renewal. Evans publishes a monthly newsletter called *The Urban Alternative,* in which, not long ago, there appeared an article entitled "10 Steps to Urban Renewal." It mentioned sound Bible teaching, rejection of government dependence, use of spiritual gifts, the discipling of converts, and other things. One important requirement, according to Evans, is becoming a community. He wrote, "The church is first and foremost a spiritual family, a community. That's why the Bible refers to the church as a 'household of faith,' 'family of God' and 'brothers and sisters.' It's meant to function as a family, model family life, and care for the families it encompasses."[6]

The church can do that as no other organization can—not businesses, not schools, not the centers of entertainment or social life, not government or city agencies. Only the church! Moreover, the church has an extraordinary opportunity to model community at a time when other forms of true community are breaking down. There is no better place than the fellowship of Christians for embracing those suffering from ruptured marriages, fractured homes, and other broken relationships.

If we can model attractive Christian community in a Christian or church setting, we can model it in other environments, as Christians in business show what it is to have a Christ-centered business. Christians in education show what it is to educate in a Christian way, politicians to act as Christian politicians, and so on in the other professions.

3. We must be a biblical community. This leads to the third necessary ingredient for an effective Christian presence in the city. Not only must we be in the city and be a community, but we must also be Bible directed. In other words, we must be the kind of community God wants us to be. What kind of a community is that? This is a big subject, of course, but a short statement of it is found in Micah: "What does the LORD require of you? To act justly and to love mercy and to walk humbly with your God" (Mic. 6:8).

That verse lists three requirements. First, to act justly. This means justice for all, not just for Christians or for our pet projects. It means justice for the Jew and the Catholic, the homosexual, the poor and the rich, the utterly destitute. Justice is impartial. It means acting justly, not just talking about justice. It means acting justly ourselves and not just expecting other people to do it.

Second, to love mercy. This does not mean we should merely act in a compassionate way from time to time, still less only to those who are like us or not much worse off than us. It means trying to show mercy always and in all possible ways. The activities of city Christians can be just and merciful at the same time.

Third, to walk humbly with God. We especially need to hear this since often Christians are anything but humble. Instead of working with others in a genuinely humble manner, we act as if we already have all the answers (which we do not) and thus rightly cause the secular world to scorn us.

4. We need a vision. The final element needed for an effective Christian presence in the city is a vision for the kind of society we hope to see established. Up to this point, we have failed in providing our secular culture with this vision. Colonel V. Doner, in a recent book entitled *The Samaritan Strategy: A New Agenda for Christian Activism*, claims that this was the specific failure of the Christian Right in the 1980s. It was able to marshal effective support for a few select causes, such as the fight against abortion or pornography. But it had no vision for the kind of society we should want to see established. The Christian Right was regarded as a crusade only for Christian interests as well as a threat to those who had even slightly different goals.

Writes Doner:

> To many, it appeared that all the Christian Right had to offer was a negative/ reactionary collage of "don'ts" rather than a comprehensive and constructive agenda of "dos." Worse yet, most Christians could not understand how all the issues connected to each other. . . . Without a clear Christian worldview, Christians were unable to act in unison behind a comprehensive and clearly understood agenda.[7]

That carefully thought-out and well-articulated Christian worldview has not yet emerged. Developing such a vision should be a primary objective for our time.

And while we are doing that, we should not think that the world is utterly opposed to us. The society about is far less hostile than we sometimes think. Not long ago the Gallup Poll organization conducted a survey of residents of cities with populations that exceed fifty thousand, asking what organizations they perceived as trying hardest to improve city life. There were all kinds of suggestions: the mayor, city council, local newspapers, local businesses, neighborhood groups, the chamber of commerce, banks, service clubs, builders, almost anything you can think of. Do you know what group led the list? The local churches! They gained 48 percent of the vote, ahead of even the mayor, who came in second. And he had only 39 percent.

Let's not be negative. The world is waiting to see what true Christians can do. I think even God is waiting. Ray Bakke has written, "I think God wants to bless [the] cities, and he waits for a renewed church."[8]

13

The Dedication of the Wall

Nehemiah 12:27–47

At the dedication of the wall of Jerusalem, the Levites were sought out from where they lived and were brought to Jerusalem to celebrate joyfully the dedication with songs of thanksgiving and with the music of cymbals, harps and lyres. The singers also were brought together from the region around Jerusalem—from the villages of the Netophathites, from Beth Gilgal, and from the area of Geba and Azmaveth, for the singers had built villages for themselves around Jerusalem. When the priests and Levites had purified themselves ceremonially, they purified the people, the gates and the wall.

I had the leaders of Judah go up on top of the wall. I also assigned two large choirs to give thanks. One was to proceed on top of the wall to the right, toward the Dung Gate. . . .

The second choir proceeded in the opposite direction. I followed them on top of the wall, together with half the people. . . .

The two choirs that gave thanks then took their places in the house of God; so did I, together with half the officials, as well as the priests—Eliakim, Maaseiah, Miniamin, Micaiah, Elioenai, Zechariah and Hananiah with their trumpets—and also Maaseiah, Shemaiah, Eleazar, Uzzi, Jehohanan, Malkijah, Elam and Ezer. The choirs sang under the direction of Jezrahiah. And on that day they offered great sacrifices, rejoicing because God had given them great joy. The women and children also rejoiced. The sound of rejoicing in Jerusalem could be heard far away.

At that time men were appointed to be in charge of the storerooms for the contributions, firstfruits and tithes. . . .

Nehemiah 12:27–31, 38, 40–44

The Christian life is hard work. Even the Bible recognizes it as hard work by describing it as a battle ("Fight the good fight of the faith" [1 Tim. 6:12]), a race ("I have finished the race" [2 Tim. 4:7]), and a sacrifice ("I urge you, brothers, in view of God's mercy, to offer your bodies as living sacrifices, holy and pleasing to God—this is your spiritual act of worship" [Rom. 12:1]). Bible study is hard. Prayer is hard. Witnessing is hard. Living a holy life in the midst of the temptations of this world is extremely difficult. Because of these difficulties, perhaps we can be excused if, from time to time in our struggles, we tend to regard the Christian life as an example of what Winston Churchill promised England at the start of World War II: a life of "blood, sweat and tears," more than a joy and triumph.

The Christian life is a struggle, of course. Jesus promised his followers not a comfortable life but a cross. But it is not only that! After times of struggle, there are often pleasant times of sweet rest. After warfare there is victory. Along with the groans of spiritual exertion, there are times of joyous celebration.

We come to one great example of celebration in Nehemiah 12, which tells of the dedication of the wall of Jerusalem. We do not know exactly when this dedication occurred, but it cannot have been long after the events of the previous chapters, since Nehemiah was a practical, hard-driving man who would not have delayed this climax to the achievements of the beginning of his governorship of Judah for more than a month at most. He had completed the wall within fifty-two days of his arrival in Jerusalem, on September 21, 444 BC. He had delayed the wall's dedication until the important festivals of the seventh month could be observed. But these were now behind him; the revival and rededication of the people had been achieved, and he called the people together for a celebration.

The narrative tells how Nehemiah brought the Levites, musicians, and singers in from the outlying regions of the country, took the people up on the wall, and staged a great procession or parade. It had two parts. One part was led by Nehemiah and proceeded in one direction around the wall while the other part was led by Ezra and proceeded in the other direction around the wall. Each group was led by musicians and choirs that sang praises to God and gave thanks to him. Then, after the circumference of the wall had been navigated in this manner, the people converged at the temple, offered sacrifices, and rejoiced so loudly that "the sound of rejoicing in Jerusalem could be heard far away" (v. 43).

A Climax to the Book

Some people have wondered why the account of the dedication of the wall of Jerusalem has been held until now and not inserted at the end of chapter 6, where we were first told that the wall was finished. It could have been fitted in there, of course. But if it had been inserted there, it would not have been the fitting climax to the entire book that it is, nor would the book have demonstrated such a meaningful unity.

Let me explain.

Remember that the book has two parts. The first and longer part concerns the building of the walls, a task in which Nehemiah played the leading role. This part fills chapters 1–7. The second, shorter part concerns the revival in Jerusalem and the rededication of the people. In this revival Ezra, the priest and spiritual head of the nation, is most prominent. This part occupies chapters 8:1–12:26. In the dedication of the walls, these two important sections of the book come together. Ezra is present to lead one-half of the celebrating people. Nehemiah leads the other. Moreover—and this is most significant—the two groups circle the walls, which Nehemiah had built, and converge at the temple, the spiritual center of the nation's life at which Ezra presides.

One commentator says this: "When the people march on the walls to the Temple they do so *after* having placed the *Temple* once again at the center of their thoughts (10:32–39). The walls thus appear for what they are: not a monument to the strength of Judah—heaven forbid!—but God's gift for the protection and perpetuation of his name in the world."[1]

It is significant that with the section beginning at verse 27 (specifically at v. 31) the first-person narrative style, which was followed in the first half of the book, is resumed again. The meaning seems to be that Nehemiah rightly assumed a backseat while Ezra the priest led in the renewal and rededication of the people, but now, as the rededicated people were prepared to dedicate the walls, Nehemiah reassumed the leading role. It was certainly appropriate that he led in the dedication of the walls, since he had been the chief mover in their reconstruction.

A List of Accomplishments

What a great list of accomplishments lay behind Nehemiah as he came to the climax of this first year of his triumphant governorship of Judah! The list is so impressive that it is worth reviewing it.

1. Nehemiah secured Artaxerxes' permission to rebuild the walls of the desolated city. This was not so easy an achievement as it might seem. One obstacle was Nehemiah's position at the court. He was useful to Artaxerxes, and it was not to be expected that the king would willingly release him for a task in a distant land. More formidable than this, however, was the fact that Nehemiah was asking the king to reverse a previously established policy regarding Jerusalem. There had already been an earlier attempt to rebuild the walls under Ezra. But when the leaders of the cities around Jerusalem saw what was happening, they petitioned Artaxerxes against the project (Ezra 4:11–16), and Artaxerxes stopped it. It was this same king whom Nehemiah had to ask to let him rebuild the walls.

Nehemiah prevailed in this attempt, as we know. His success was due in part to his wisdom in approaching Artaxerxes, but chiefly to his dependence on God, which he showed by his approach to God in prayer. Throughout the narrative, Nehemiah is seen to be a man of prayer.

2. Nehemiah developed a plan for constructing the walls. Part of his plan involved advance preparation in which he arranged with the king to be provided with the necessary supplies. The other part of the plan emerged as a result of his nocturnal inspection of the ruins. It was no small objective—to reassemble huge stones into a one-and-a-half- or two-and-a-half-mile-long fortification around the ruined city. But Nehemiah worked out how it could be done and launched the project.

3. Nehemiah inspired a defeated and dispirited people. Not only was the objective itself overwhelming, but Nehemiah also had to cope with a people who had tried to build the walls before, had failed, and were now dispirited. There had been nearly a century of defeat. The people had settled down into accepting things as they were. Somehow Nehemiah inspired this dispirited people to believe the job could be done.

This is the area in which a leader shows whether or not he really is a leader. If a leader cannot inspire, people will not follow. If they do not follow, the leader is a leader in name only. Nehemiah was not only a leader nominally. He really led the people, and his leadership began by his success in inspiring them to believe that what he had come to Jerusalem to accomplish was possible—and that it was possible through them.

4. Nehemiah overcame a bewildering barrage of opposition, some from his enemies without and some from his own people within. After the project got under way, Nehemiah was opposed by many people and in a variety of ways. The first two forms of opposition were from Sanballat the Horonite, the ruler of Samaria to the north, and Tobiah the Ammonite. The first type of opposition was ridicule. The second was the threat of violence. Nehemiah overcame the first by committing the matter to God and by keeping on with the work. He overcame the second by such practical matters as arming the people, posting guards, and rearranging work assignments to be prepared for surprise attacks. He kept reminding the people that God was with them.

Suddenly Nehemiah was faced with a bigger and potentially even more damaging problem: corruption from within the nation itself. Some of the wealthier Jews were taking advantage of their less prosperous brothers and sisters. In this case, Nehemiah actually stopped the work to sort out the problem. He knew there was no point in defending the people by walls if what was going on behind the walls was not worth defending.

The final three forms of opposition again came from the people's external enemies, Sanballat and Tobiah among others. These differed from the first types of opposition in that they were directed against Nehemiah personally. A plot was hatched that was intended to compromise him. A rumor campaign was started. Finally there was an attempt at outright intimidation. Nehemiah overcame these attacks through five great qualities: (1) he was close to God, (2) he had a strong sense of God's calling, (3) he had a healthy sense of his own abilities and worth, (4) he had discernment, and (5) he had courage. God used these qualities to see Nehemiah through the attack of his enemies and enable him to press forward to victory.

5. *Nehemiah completed the reconstruction of the wall.* What a great accomplishment and triumph this was! He did in just fifty-two days what others had been unable to do in almost a century.

6. *Nehemiah encouraged and assisted in a national revival.* His achievement here was twofold. First, he saw the need for revival where a lesser man might have been content with his own personal and external accomplishment—the building of the wall. Second, he realized that someone else, Ezra, was better positioned to lead the revival, so he stepped aside until this phase of the work, led by Ezra, was accomplished. A lesser man would have been unwilling to do this.

7. *Nehemiah reorganized and repopulated the city.* The last in this list of accomplishments was the implementation of a plan to repopulate the city of Jerusalem. It was after he had completed this—with the walls, the temple, the religious and civil leaders, and the masses of the people all in place—that Nehemiah proceeded with the wall's dedication.

Few people have had as much to celebrate after a lifetime of hard work as Nehemiah had after less than a year as Judah's governor.

The Dedication of the People

In the eighth chapter of 2 Corinthians, the apostle Paul is writing about the surprising generosity of the Christians in Macedonia, asking how they had managed to be so generous when they were actually quite poor. His explanation is that "they gave themselves first to the Lord and then to us in keeping with God's will" (v. 5). That is a secret for spiritual success: to give ourselves to God first, and then to others. There was something like this in the dedication of the walls of Jerusalem, at least in the sense that the people dedicated themselves to God before they dedicated the gates, the wall, or the city.

What is a dedication? The word comes from the Latin verb *do, dare, dedi, datum,* which means "to offer" or "to give." When an object is dedicated—to the Lord, for example—it means it is given to him for his control and use. When a person dedicates herself or himself to God, it is for the same reason.

In Nehemiah 12, the priests and Levites were the first to dedicate (or, as it says, "purify") themselves, which was fitting since they were the ones who were to conduct the dedication service. We are not told what this work of purification consisted of, but it was probably ceremonial washings of themselves and their clothes, fasting, abstinence from sexual intercourse, and sin offerings.[2]

The people were next. They probably merely washed themselves and their clothing,[3] though they may have been asked to abstain from sexual relations too.[4]

The gates and wall would have been dedicated by using a hyssop brush to sprinkle them with the blood of sacrifices and with water.[5]

The Dedication of the Great Wall

After we are told about the dedication of the people, followed by a ceremonial sprinkling of the gates and wall, we are told of the great service of dedication itself. As I indicated above, it consisted of two parts: (1) a festive wall-walk, in which Nehemiah led one group of people in one direction while Ezra led a second group of people in the other direction, and (2) a formal service at the temple at which the choirs sang and the priests offered sacrifices.

In my opinion, the details of what took place in these services are less significant than the spirit in which they were conducted. And when I think of the celebration in terms of this overall spirit, I notice two very important things:

1. Singing. According to Nehemiah's account, the chief place in these services was given to the choirs and the instrumentalists—the players of "cymbals, harps and lyres" (v. 27). These led each of the two groups around the wall, the choirs no doubt singing all the way. And then, when the service was ready to begin, the choirs took their places first and led the singing. The music was so important to the occasion that the name of the choir director is recorded. His name was Jezrahiah.

What did the people sing? The psalms, certainly. We do not know which ones, of course. But I would be surprised if they did not sing the psalms that chronicle God's blessing to the people in past days: Psalms 78, 105, and 106. Or the psalms of ascent (Psalms 120–134), which were written for pilgrims who were making their way up to Jerusalem to worship.

Or how could they have missed Psalm 48, with its final stanza describing what they were in the very act of doing:

> Walk about Zion, go around her,
>   count her towers,
> consider well her ramparts,

view her citadels,
   that you may tell of them to the next generation.
For this God is our God for ever and ever;
   he will be our guide even to the end.

verses 12–14

Charles Swindoll makes a great deal of the importance of singing in the Christian life in his study of this chapter, and I think he is right in doing so. Singing has always been a striking feature of the worship of God's Old Testament and New Testament people. This is not true of other religions. Many use repetitive chants. In some, clergy sing. But generally the religions of the world are grim things. It is only in biblical religion that the people of God are characteristically joyful and express their joy in great singing.

Christians write hymns. They sing them in their services.

Christians write choruses, and although the sentiments and music of some of them may be theologically and aesthetically dreadful, they are nevertheless generally joyful.

Christian musicians compose great oratorios.

Why is this? Obviously because Christianity is itself joyous. It is a response to the great acts of God on our behalf, particularly in the life, death, and resurrection of Jesus Christ, which secured our salvation.

No wonder we sing:

> Joy to the world! The Lord is come!
> Let earth receive her King:
> Let every heart prepare Him room,
> And heaven and nature sing.

We sing hymns about the Lord's resurrection:

> Jesus Christ is risen today, Alleluia!
> Our triumphant holy day, Alleluia!
> Who did once upon the cross, Alleluia!
> Suffer to redeem our loss. Alleluia!

We sing about his ascension and exaltation:

> Crown him with many crowns,
> The Lamb upon his throne.

And his return:

> Thou art coming, O my Saviour,
> Thou art coming, O my King,

In thy beauty all resplendent;
In thy glory all transcendent;
Well may we rejoice and sing:
Coming! in the opening east
Herald brightness slowly swells;
Coming! O my glorious Priest,
Hear we not thy golden bells?

Christians sing on all occasions, even at funerals. One of the most thrilling song experiences I have had has been standing at the graveside of a deceased member of the Tenth Presbyterian Church congregation while the family and friends sang together:

On Christ, the solid Rock, I stand;
All other ground is sinking sand.

2. *Rejoicing.* The second thing I notice about the celebration services at the dedication of Jerusalem's wall is the rejoicing. This is related to what I have been saying about singing, since the best singing flows from a rejoicing heart. But singing can also be sad. Some hymns have a sad or melancholy tone. Since rejoicing is emphasized in Nehemiah 13, we are to understand that on this occasion the singing in Jerusalem was all of a joyful nature.

This element is emphasized more than any other. Verse 43 is the climax of the story, and it is striking that the root of the Hebrew word for *joy* or *rejoicing* occurs five times in just this one verse. What a contrast to Ezra 3:12–13, which tells of weeping on the part of the older returned exiles at the dedication service for the foundation of the temple. The older people remembered the former temple, which Nebuchadnezzar had destroyed, and unfavorably contrasted the new foundation to it.

There was nothing like that now. The text says, "And on that day they offered great sacrifices, rejoicing because God had given them great joy. The women and children also rejoiced. The sound of rejoicing in Jerusalem could be heard far away" (Neh. 12:43).

I want to note one more thing about that verse. There is a fourfold repetition of the words *joy* and *rejoice.* But notice that it is not merely said that the people felt joyful or were enjoying themselves but that this was "because God had given them great joy." Their joy was spiritual and not just a hedonistic thing. It was exactly what Paul was to speak of later in writing to the Philippians: "Rejoice *in the Lord* always. I will say it again: Rejoice!" (Phil. 4:4, italics added).

J. G. McConville says:

If the joy of Nehemiah's Jerusalem seems alien and Paul's unnatural, it is simply a measure of the difficulty experienced by a rich western world in finding well-being in godliness itself. What Nehemiah and Paul knew—in direct contrast to the modern doctrine that he who acquires most and succeeds best is happiest—is that joy, like love, peace, self-control, etc. (cf. Gal. 5:22), is *spiritual*.[6]

The Work Goes On

There is one more thing. Strictly speaking, the account of the dedication of the wall of Jerusalem ends with verse 43. But in Nehemiah's mind (since he is telling the story), the account does not really end there but continues with (1) the appointment of men to be in charge of the storerooms for the temple and the provision of supplies for the services (Neh. 12:44–47) and (2) the continuing purification of the people by excluding from their official number all who were of foreign descent (Neh. 13:1–3).

Nehemiah very carefully links those acts to the time of the dedication by using the words "at that time" of the first (12:44) and the word "on that day" of the second (13:1).

It is not difficult to apply this. It means that the times of rejoicing, though important, are not ends in themselves but are meant to be additional ongoing moments in the lives of those who have given themselves to God. Rejoice in God? Of course! We above all other people should rejoice in God. In fact, only those who have been redeemed by the Lord Jesus Christ have any real and deep cause for rejoicing. But that is not all we have to do. We have work to do too, and we must get on with it.

In fact, we are going to see that even Nehemiah had to get on with it. Although he had rebuilt both the wall and the nation, he was to find that rebuilding the nation was not something that could be done once for all and then be neglected. On the contrary, he had to tackle it all again years later when he was sent to Judah a second time. The final chapter of Nehemiah reports what he did then.

14

The Eighth Dynamic:
Nehemiah's Final Reforms

Nehemiah 13:1–31

On that day the Book of Moses was read aloud in the hearing of the people and there it was found written that no Ammonite or Moabite should ever be admitted into the assembly of God, because they had not met the Israelites with food and water but had hired Balaam to call a curse down on them. (Our God, however, turned the curse into a blessing.) When the people heard this law, they excluded from Israel all who were of foreign descent.

Before this, Eliashib the priest had been put in charge of the storerooms of the house of our God. He was closely associated with Tobiah, and he had provided him with a large room formerly used to store the grain offerings and incense and temple articles, and also the tithes of grain, new wine and oil prescribed for the Levites, singers and gatekeepers, as well as the contributions for the priests.

But while all this was going on, I was not in Jerusalem, for in the thirty-second year of Artaxerxes king of Babylon I had returned to the king. Some time later I asked his permission and came back to Jerusalem. Here I learned about the evil thing Eliashib had done in providing Tobiah a room in the court of the house of God. I was greatly displeased and threw all Tobiah's household goods out of the room. I gave orders to purify the rooms, and then I put back into them the equipment of the house of God, with the grain offerings and the incense.

I also learned that the portions assigned to the Levites had not been given to them, and that all the Levites and singers responsible for the service had gone back to their own fields. So I rebuked the officials and asked them, "Why is the house of God neglected?" Then I called them together and stationed them at their posts. . . .

In those days I saw men in Judah treading winepresses on the Sabbath and bringing in grain and loading it on donkeys, together with wine, grapes, figs and all other kinds of loads. And they were bringing all this into Jerusalem on the Sabbath. . . .

When evening shadows fell on the gates of Jerusalem before the Sabbath, I ordered the doors to be shut and not opened until the Sabbath was over. . . .

Moreover, in those days I saw men of Judah who had married women from Ashdod, Ammon and Moab. Half of their children spoke the language of Ashdod or the language of one of the other peoples, and did not know how to speak the language of Judah. I rebuked them and called curses down on them. I beat some of the men and pulled out their hair. I made them take an oath in God's name and said: "You are not to give your daughters in marriage to their sons, nor are you to take their daughters in marriage for your sons or for yourselves." . . .

Remember me with favor, O my God.

Nehemiah 13:1–11, 15, 19, 23–25, 31

I begin this final study of Nehemiah with the history of a well-known politician. I wonder if you can identify him. He was born in 1809 and suffered his first major defeat in 1832, a year in which he lost his job and was defeated in his first political race, a bid for the state legislature. The next year, 1833, he failed in business. In 1835 his childhood sweetheart died. In 1836 he had a nervous breakdown. In 1843 he was defeated in a bid for the United States Congress. In 1848 he tried again and was again defeated. In 1849 he decided to become a land officer but was rejected. In 1854 he was defeated in a race for the United States Senate. In 1856 he lost a nomination for the vice presidency. In 1858 he was again defeated in a race for the Senate.

A list of defeats like this would be enough to discourage any man, but he said, "I will always do my best no matter what . . . and someday my chance will come." One day it did. In 1861, Abraham Lincoln became the sixteenth president of the United States.[1]

Perseverance! It is a mark of true leadership.

Sir Winston Churchill, another great leader, once said, "Never give up. Never, never, never give up." It could have been a summary of the life of Nehemiah.

Even Down to Old Age

Nehemiah did not have the series of defeats in his life by which Abraham Lincoln was provided and strengthened. But he would have understood at once what Lincoln and Churchill believed about perseverance. Nehemiah was a whirlwind leader, as we have seen. But he did not merely do his own thing and then move on to be remembered no more. On the contrary, he kept fighting his battles to the very end. One commentator says, "To the end of his days Nehemiah retained the same zeal that mobilized the laws to rebuild the walls and that made him intervene earlier to abolish exploitation of the poor. Nehemiah was not a flash-in-the-pan leader but one who remained as long as he lived, consistent to his original vision."[2]

Because this last chapter of Nehemiah is about perseverance, in some ways it is the most important chapter in the book.

To begin with, Nehemiah 13 concerns a time somewhat removed from the first chapters. The time indication is in verse 6, where Nehemiah explains that he had returned to Babylon in the thirty-second year of Artaxerxes and that what he is recounting now was "some time later." It appears from this that Nehemiah had two governorships of Judah. The first, which he has described in Nehemiah 5:14, extended from the twentieth to the thirty-second year of Artaxerxes. That is, it lasted for twelve years, from 445 BC to 433 BC. Some commentators consider it unlikely that Nehemiah spent all twelve of those years in Judah, judging that he must have returned to Babylon shortly after the victories of his first great year and perhaps only returned intermittently during the twelve-year period. But Nehemiah does not say this. On the contrary, the gap in which the problems of chapter 13 developed seems to have been between the end of his first twelve-year assignment and the second assignment years later.

How many years was this? There is no way of knowing, since Nehemiah is vague. Presumably a considerable period of time elapsed, since the problems of the final chapter are major ones and would not have happened overnight. Guesses for the year of Nehemiah's return to Jerusalem run from 425 BC[3] to 420 BC,[4] dates near the end of the reign of King Artaxerxes.

The significant thing is that Nehemiah was now considerably older. He must have been at least forty when he left Susa for Jerusalem the first time. The end of his first governorship would have brought him to the age of fifty-two, and if we are now in the years 425 to 420 BC, Nehemiah must have been near sixty-five. This is the age at which most people today retire. But Nehemiah did not retire. In this chapter we see him returning to Jerusalem and achieving some of his most important victories.

The Same Old Problems

It is not just that Nehemiah had to continue his struggles into old age that is significant. It is also that he had to deal with exactly the same problems he had dealt with earlier.

In the last chapter, we looked at the climactic celebration in which Nehemiah, together with Ezra the priest, dedicated the wall of the newly encircled city. At the very end of that study, we saw something interesting. Two sections deal with: (1) the provisions made for the temple service (Neh. 12:44–47) and (2) the purification of the people by excluding from their official number all who were of foreign descent (Neh. 13:1–3). Some commentators have called these sections parenthetical, but that is not how Nehemiah viewed them. He links these sections to the dedication by using the phrases "at that time" and "on that day," though what they describe was probably spread out over a period of weeks or months. It is his way of saying that the purity of the people and the religious life of the nation were the ultimate goal and the very heart of what he was striving to accomplish.

These were the problems he faced when he returned to the city some seven or twelve years later. His second governorship did not deal with a new set of problems but with the old ones. If you have ever had a similar experience, you know it is enough to grind down even the best of leaders.

And there is this too. Do you remember the covenant made by the people at the time of the religious revival under Ezra, recorded in Nehemiah 10? The revival had three parts. There was a reading and exposition of the Law of God, which led to the conviction of sin (chap. 8). There was national repentance for wrongs done (chap. 9). Finally, there was a covenant in which the people promised to obey the commands of God faithfully (chap. 10). Do you remember what they covenanted to?

There were six items:

1. The family. The people promised not to intermarry with the people of the nations about them. This was not racial snobbery or prejudice, as I pointed out earlier. It was a desire to preserve their religion and the unique quality of the spiritual life that flowed from it.

2. The Sabbath. The people promised to abstain from all commercial activity on this day, preserving it as a day to worship God and remember his blessings.

3. The temple tax. The people promised to pay the tax required of them by Exodus 30:11–16. They took it as an annual obligation.

4. Additional provisions for the temple. The people were not content merely with paying the tax for the temple but also promised to provide the temple with wood for the altar and the firstfruits of their crops and trees.

5. Dedication of the firstborn. This was a matter of priorities. It was a way of acknowledging that all we are and have is a gift from God and is owed to him.

6. The tithe. The final thing the people promised was to be faithful in paying tithes to God. The tithe was paid to the Levites, and the Levites paid a tithe of all they received to the priests. This was the way the people provided for the temple service.

But it was exactly this that Nehemiah found to have been neglected when he returned for his second period as governor in 425 or 420 BC. In fact, of the six items solemnly covenanted in chapter 10, the only one that does not recur in chapter 13 is the obligation to dedicate the firstborn to God, and that is probably because it is subsumed under the greater problem of the family and intermarriages with foreign peoples dealt with extensively in verses 22–28. How pious the people were in promising these things in the revival! How solemnly they declared, "We will not neglect the house of our God" (Neh. 10:39). But they did neglect it. They broke their promises.

Perhaps the people had simply forgotten these things or didn't really understand what was required.

No, that will not do. During the years of Nehemiah's absence from Jerusalem, God sent Malachi, the last of the Old Testament prophets, to inveigh against these very abuses. He chided them for shoddy worship (Mal. 1:6–14), a corrupt priesthood (Mal. 2:1–9), marriage with foreigners (Mal. 2:10–16), and robbing God by neglecting to pay the tithe (Mal. 3:6–12). Since Malachi had been calling for reform and a return to God in these very areas, it is reasonable to think that Nehemiah faced problems not only of a backslidden people but of hardened hearts as well.

A Worm in the Big Apple

These problems were dramatically illustrated by what Nehemiah found going on at the temple. Eliashib, the high priest (v. 28) with whom he had worked closely during his earlier governorship and whom he had placed in charge of the temple storerooms, had affiliated himself with Tobiah the Ammonite, Nehemiah's old enemy (vv. 4–5). Later we learn that Eliashib had also given a daughter in marriage to Nehemiah's other archenemy, Sanballat the Horonite of Samaria (v. 28). Here we are told that he had provided Tobiah with rooms in the temple, putting him in a suite of rooms where the temple articles, tithes, and offerings had formerly been stored.

Why had Eliashib done it? Probably because, as he would have said, "We are living in a new day. Nehemiah has returned to Babylon. His old style of aggressive leadership was all right in the past, but it is not politically astute for this time. What we need today is compromise, a building of bridges, a handout to old friends."

We can be sure that Tobiah had been working his side of the alliance too. He would have been maneuvering for entree into the highest leadership positions in the city. Tobiah had a Jewish name, and when Nehemiah had first come to Jerusalem, he discovered (and reports) that Tobiah had married the daughter of Shecaniah son of Arah, one of the leaders of the city, and that his daughter had married Meshullam son of Berekiah, another leader (Neh. 6:18; cf. 3:4; 7:10; 10:7; 12:3, 14, 32). Tobiah would have done anything to get even a toehold in the city. He must have been delighted with the splendid arrangements Eliashib made for him. In the temple precincts, he had a base from which to ferment intrigue and increase his bad influence.

In my opinion, one of the very best sections of the book comes next. When Nehemiah got back to Jerusalem and discovered what had been done, he wasted not the slightest bit of time either in investigation or negotiation. He simply threw Tobiah and all his possessions out! He dumped his possessions outside the door onto the sidewalk, fumigated the room, and then restored the temple articles. Just like that!

Was Nehemiah angry? He was. He says he was "greatly displeased" (v. 8), and he showed it.

Was he right to be angry? The answer is yes to that too.

As we noted earlier, many Christians are uneasy with anger, and some have not hesitated to criticize Nehemiah at this point. They are forgetting a few things. First, Nehemiah's angry cleansing of the temple is a foretaste of the similar action taken later by Jesus Christ. Jesus was angry, and he was not wrong to be so.

Second, although he was displeased with Eliashib and calls what he had done "the evil thing," Nehemiah is not as outspoken in condemning the evil of these days as God had already been through Malachi. Malachi had said that God was sending a curse on this priesthood (Mal. 2:2). Indeed, his whole prophecy is a denunciation of the evils for which spiritual leaders like Eliashib were responsible.

Third, critics of Nehemiah forget that deep-seated wrongs are seldom corrected except by people who have first become sufficiently angry. The cool, the complacent, the compromisers don't change anything.

It is possible to be wrongly angry, of course. That is often the case when a wrong only against ourselves is involved. We can be wrong if we do nothing more than get angry. Righteous anger, the kind God approves of, always acts to correct the injustice. But wrong anger is not our major problem in today's Christianity. The bigger problems are compromise and cowardice. John White says:

> In Christian work our cowardice in avoiding unpleasantness is currently doing more damage than any damage from irascibility on the part of Christian leaders. And what irascibility we do give way to is usually verbal. It wounds without correcting. The church has become flabby, old womanish, inept, unwilling to act. Discipline should be reconciliatory and loving, *but it should take place.* And on the whole it doesn't. . . . Who are we—who condone every manner of evil in our midst—to criticize one of those rare leaders who does not hesitate to act when the integrity of God's temple is in question?[5]

Apparently, Nehemiah did not fear to place his actions before God for judgment, for he says in verse 14, "Remember me for this, O my God, and do not blot out what I have so faithfully done for the house of my God and its services." We should all be so bold!

Nehemiah's Final Reforms

After dealing with the erring Eliashib and Tobiah, Nehemiah moved with the same determination to right the other wrongs he discovered. These wrongs correspond to the items promised by the people in chapter 10. Nehemiah's actions in dealing with them constitute his final reforms.

1. The tithe (vv. 10–11). Nehemiah learned that the tithes for the temple service had not been paid and that the Levites and singers responsible for the temple worship had therefore left Jerusalem and gone back to their own fields to earn a living. Probably there was a connection between this problem and the earlier one. If Eliashib the high priest was acting in an unprincipled manner, the people had probably begun to lose confidence in the priestly establishment, and it is understandable that the tithes would be neglected. On the other hand, the tithe obligation remained for the people regardless of the spiritual quality of the leadership; the tithe was a biblical command. It is probably true that the people were just neglecting this responsibility.

Nehemiah dealt with this problem through the proper officials, since the responsibility for collecting the tithe was theirs. He rebuked them, reinstated the Levites in their position, and reestablished the system for collecting tithes.

2. Other provisions for the temple (vv. 12–13). Additional provisions for the temple had also suffered, no doubt for the same reasons as the neglect of the tithe. Nehemiah moved to correct this abuse too. He dismissed the old custodians, who would have been in tight with Eliashib, and installed Shelemiah, Zadok, Pedaiah, and Hanan in their places "because these men were considered trustworthy" (v. 13).

The mention of Zadok as "the scribe" may be important. There could have been any number of scribes, of course. But since he is called *"the* scribe" and since no one but Ezra has been called "the scribe" before this, it is reasonable to assume either that Ezra was no longer in the city (perhaps he had returned to Babylon) or was too old to officiate (he had been in Jerusalem even longer than Nehemiah) or had died.

3. The Sabbath (vv. 15–22). The longest single section of Nehemiah 13 deals with the desecration of the Sabbath. Like a trickle through a dike, commercial activity on the Sabbath had probably begun slowly—in the countryside with the farmers harvesting grain and treading grapes. But it had grown steadily stronger. Having harvested their grain and made their wine, the farmers next brought these to the city to be sold—again on the Sabbath. Following quickly on their heels were traders from Tyre who had fish and "all kinds of merchandise" for the markets.

Nehemiah did four things that were typical of his leadership style.

First, he rebuked the nobles who were responsible for the city's life, warning them that it was for such abuses the judgment of God had come on the people years before. It was characteristic of Nehemiah to work through those who were officially in charge.

Second, he locked the gates on the Sabbath, placing some of his own men over them. This was a practical device by a practical man. If the gates could not be opened, it was certain that no merchandise would flow into the city through them.

Third, when the merchants (probably the merchants from Tyre) camped outside Jerusalem hoping for a change in the Sabbath regulations or perhaps looking for a way to get around them, Nehemiah threatened them with forceful action if they did not move on. He did not even want temptation to be hanging around the perimeter of the Jewish city.

Finally, Nehemiah instructed the Levites to purify themselves and then take over the task of guarding the city gates on the Sabbath. He wanted this to be their responsibility, and he knew he and his men would not always be around to do it for them.

After telling what he did to restore the Sabbath, Nehemiah appeals to God in the second of four similar prayers in this chapter: "Remember me for this also, O my God, and show mercy to me according to your great love" (v. 22).

4. *The family* (vv. 23–28). The final abuse was an old one, going back to the people's early days in the land: intermarriage with the nations round-about, the very thing they had promised to avoid in chapter 10. Half of the children of these marriages did not even know how to speak the Jews' language, according to Nehemiah, and the problem had extended upward into the families of even the leaders of the city. As Nehemiah explains in verse 28, a grandson of Eliashib the high priest had married a daughter of Sanballat the Horonite.

In this case, Nehemiah did not act as radically as Ezra had done earlier when he required the Jewish men to divorce their foreign wives (Ezra 9–10). Nevertheless, he gave them a thorough dressing-down and publicly humiliated some of them, extracting renewed promises that the people would abstain from damaging marriages with foreign peoples (v. 25). As for the grandson of Eliashib, Nehemiah simply drove him from the city.

Thus ended the last of these reforms.

Nehemiah closes with two more prayers: one against those who corrupted the priesthood ("Remember them, O my God, because they defiled the priestly office and the covenant of the priesthood and of the Levites" [v. 29]) and one for himself ("Remember me with favor, O my God" [v. 31]).

Four Leadership Characteristics

I am sure, Nehemiah's prayer to the contrary, that God did not need to be urged to remember this great leader. He had obeyed God nobly, and for many centuries he has been enjoying his reward. It is we who need to be urged to remember him. We need to remember his faith and his great leadership characteristics. Of the many we have seen, I have been most impressed with the following:

1. Nehemiah's submission to God. Nehemiah had no other plans for his life than to do what God had for him. He could have said with Jesus, "Not as I will, but as you will" (Matt. 26:39).

2. Nehemiah's ability to focus on the right goals. Nehemiah clearly saw the ultimate goals and the objectives leading to them. He never deviated from any of them, even for a moment.

3. Nehemiah's wisdom in handling complex situations. The problems Nehemiah faced were all different, and the solution to one was not the solution to another. Nehemiah did not have rote answers. He handled each problem wisely, with a wisdom that came from God.

4. Nehemiah's courage to act decisively. Because he was serving God and not man and because he knew that the purposes of God will always ultimately triumph, Nehemiah was not afraid to act boldly. His boldness left his enemies stammering, confounded, and in awe.

Evangelist Leighton Ford, brother-in-law of Billy Graham, had a son named Sandy. When he was fourteen years old, Sandy developed a heart problem from which he later died, at the age of twenty-one. For a time the problem seemed to be corrected and the young man returned to running track and cross-country, in which he excelled. On one occasion, Sandy was in a mile race, close to the tape and moving ahead to a record-setting victory with a forty-yard lead on the second-place runner. Suddenly he developed a problem in his legs, stumbled, and fell. He picked himself up, stumbled forward a few yards more, and fell again. Looking back, he saw the second-place runner closing in on him. So he got up on his hands and knees and crawled under the tape, across the finish line, and fell there, having won the race.[6]

That is perseverance. It is a quality of all great leaders. Is it true of us? We should cultivate it until we can say with the apostle Paul, "I have fought the good fight, I have finished the race, I have kept the faith. Now there is in store for me the crown of righteousness, which the Lord, the righteous Judge, will award to me on that day—and not only to me, but also to all who have longed for his appearing" (2 Tim. 4:7–8).

Remember me with favor, O my God.
                        Nehemiah 5:19

Notes

Chapter 1

1. Most books and commentaries on Nehemiah contain some of this history, but an exceptionally good account is in Howard F. Vos, *Bible Study Commentary: Ezra, Nehemiah, and Esther* (Grand Rapids: Zondervan, 1987), 10–21.

2. Peter F. Drucker, *The Effective Executive* (New York: Harper & Row, 1985), 100.

3. Quoted by Cyril J. Barber, in *Nehemiah and the Dynamics of Effective Leadership* (Neptune, NJ: Loizeaux Brothers, 1976), 19.

4. Barber, *Nehemiah and the Dynamics of Effective Leadership*, 22–23.

Chapter 2

1. Peter F. Drucker, *The Effective Executive* (New York: Harper & Row, 1985), 93.

2. Dale Carnegie, *How to Win Friends and Influence People* (New York: Simon & Schuster, 1963), 19.

3. J. G. McConville, *Ezra, Nehemiah, and Esther*, in The Daily Study Bible—Old Testament Series, ed. John C. L. Gibson (Louisville: Westminster/John Knox, 1985), 79.

4. Cyril J. Barber, *Nehemiah and the Dynamics of Effective Leadership* (Neptune, NJ: Loizeaux Brothers, 1976), 30.

5. Drucker, *Effective Executive*, 100.

6. Some commentators have questioned whether Nehemiah could have been specific about needing twelve years to rebuild the walls and reestablish Jerusalem on the grounds that Artaxerxes would not have been willing to lose a trusted servant and counselor for so long a time. They have postulated that initially Nehemiah went to Jerusalem for a period of at best a year or two, returning perhaps two or three times more over the twelve-year period (cf. Howard F. Vos, *Bible Study Commentary: Ezra, Nehemiah, and Esther* [Grand Rapids: Zondervan, 1987], 89–90; and Derek Kidner, *Ezra and Nehemiah: An Introduction*

and Commentary [Downers Grove, IL: InterVarsity Press, 1979], 81). Against this view is the fact that Nehemiah was not merely given a leave of absence from his duties in Persia but also was appointed the governor of Jerusalem, a post he would have been expected to fill for a significant period of time, and the fact that Nehemiah distinguishes between his twelve years of initial service and his final visit, described in chapter 13. Of course, he could have made trips back to Persia to report on his progress during the twelve-year governorship.

7. See Vos, *Bible Study Commentary: Ezra, Nehemiah, Esther*, 91.

Chapter 3

1. Howard F. Vos, *Bible Study Commentary: Ezra, Nehemiah, and Esther* (Grand Rapids: Zondervan, 1987), 8–9.

2. Kathleen M. Kenyon, *Jerusalem: Excavating 3000 Years of History* (New York: McGraw-Hill, 1967), 100. See also Vos, *Bible Study Commentary: Ezra, Nehemiah, Esther*, 113.

3. For details of Nehemiah's tour of the walls, see J. G. McConville, *Ezra, Nehemiah, and Esther*, in The Daily Study Bible—Old Testament Series, ed. John C. L. Gibson (Louisville: Westminster/John Knox, 1985), 83–84; Vos, *Bible Study Commentary: Ezra, Nehemiah, Esther*, 92–93; and Derek Kidner, *Ezra and Nehemiah: An Introduction and Commentary* (Downers Grove, IL: Inter-Varsity Press, 1979), 82–83.

4. Peter F. Drucker, *The Effective Executive* (New York: Harper & Row, 1985), 145–46.

5. Robert J. Schoenberg, *The Art of Being a Boss: Inside Intelligence from Top-Level Business Leaders and Young Executives on the Move* (New York: New American Library, 1980), 47, 54–58.

6. Quoted by John R. Noe, in *Peak Performance Principles for High Achievers* (New York: Frederick Fell, 1984), 134.

7. Dale Carnegie, *How to Win Friends and Influence People* (New York: Simon & Schuster, 1963), 173–76.

8. Noe, *Principles*, 6.

9. Quoted by Carnegie, in *How to Win Friends*, 175.

10. Winston S. Churchill, *Their Finest Hour*, vol. 2 of *The Second World War* (Boston: Houghton Mifflin, 1949), 25–26, 118.

11. McConville, *Ezra, Nehemiah, Esther*, 82.

Chapter 4

1. Howard F. Vos, *Bible Study Commentary: Ezra, Nehemiah, and Esther* (Grand Rapids: Zondervan, 1987), 96.

2. Quoted by John R. Noe, in *Peak Performance Principles for High Achievers* (New York: Frederick Fell, 1984), 134.

3. Peter F. Drucker, *The Effective Executive* (New York: Harper & Row, 1985), 100.

4. Robert Townsend, *Further Up the Organization* (New York: Alfred A. Knopf, 1984), 50, 55.

5. Cyril J. Barber, *Nehemiah and the Dynamics of Effective Leadership* (Neptune, NJ: Loizeaux Brothers, 1976), 50.

Chapter 5

1. Howard F. Vos, *Bible Study Commentary: Ezra, Nehemiah, and Esther* (Grand Rapids: Zondervan, 1987), 99.

2. James B. Pritchard, *Ancient Near Eastern Texts Relating to the Old Testament* (Princeton: Princeton University Press, 1955), 492.

3. Vos, *Bible Study Commentary: Ezra, Nehemiah, Esther,* 100.

4. Derek Kidner, *Ezra and Nehemiah: An Introduction and Commentary* (Downers Grove, IL: InterVarsity Press, 1979), 90.

5. This is not the place to discuss the problems the imprecatory prayers of the Old Testament create for some people, but for those who do have problems there is a helpful discussion of this prayer in Cyril J. Barber, *Nehemiah and the Dynamics of Effective Leadership* (Neptune, NJ: Loizeaux Brothers, 1976), 62–64. Barber lists three inadequate solutions: (1) that the prayer is predictive rather than imperative, (2) that it expressed Nehemiah's own wrong views rather than God's view, and (3) that it is a prayer of one who, living in the Old Testament period, has not yet been taught about grace. The answer, he feels, is in recognizing that the taunt of Sanballat and Tobiah was not so much against Nehemiah and his Jewish coworkers as it was against God. They were opposing his work. So it was right for Nehemiah to ask God to intervene in these circumstances. Nehemiah did not take vengeance himself. He was leaving the outcome to God.

Chapter 6

1. John White, *Excellence in Leadership: Reaching Goals with Prayer, Courage and Determination* (Downers Grove, IL: InterVarsity Press, 1986), 66.

2. Cyril J. Barber, *Nehemiah and the Dynamics of Effective Leadership* (Neptune, NJ: Loizeaux Brothers, 1976), 77–78.

3. White, *Excellence in Leadership,* 80–82.

4. Barber, *Nehemiah and the Dynamics of Effective Leadership,* 83–85.

5. Franky Schaeffer, *A Time for Anger: The Myth of Neutrality* (Westchester, IL: Crossway, 1982), 15.

6. From a series of tapes by Frank R. Tillapaugh entitled *Reclaiming the Church for Ministry* (Denver: Bear Valley Ministries, 1984).

7. White, *Excellence in Leadership,* 85.

Chapter 7

1. Cyril J. Barber, *Nehemiah and the Dynamics of Effective Leadership* (Neptune, NJ: Loizeaux Brothers, 1976), 97.

2. Barber, *Nehemiah and the Dynamics of Effective Leadership*, 99.

3. Quoted by Barber, in *Nehemiah and the Dynamics of Effective Leadership*, 101. Wagner's book is entitled *Put It All Together: Developing Inner Security* (Grand Rapids: Zondervan, 1974).

4. Cf. Howard F. Vos, *Bible Study Commentary: Ezra, Nehemiah, and Esther* (Grand Rapids: Zondervan, 1987), 112; and Derek Kidner, *Ezra and Nehemiah: An Introduction and Commentary* (Downers Grove, IL: InterVarsity Press, 1979), 99.

5. Barber, *Nehemiah and the Dynamics of Effective Leadership*, 108.

6. Robert Townsend, *Further Up the Organization* (New York: Alfred A. Knopf, 1948), 155.

7. Ibid., 156.

8. John White, *Excellence in Leadership: Reaching Goals with Prayer, Courage and Determination* (Downers Grove, IL: InterVarsity Press, 1986), 104.

Chapter 8

1. Cyril J. Barber, *Nehemiah and the Dynamics of Effective Leadership* (Neptune, NJ: Loizeaux Brothers, 1976), 111.

2. Although they contain virtually the same names and groupings, the two lists are nevertheless not identical. The total of individuals is the same: 42,360 (Ezra 2:64; Neh. 7:66). But the individual items add up to different and contradictory totals: 29,818 in Ezra and 31,089 in Nehemiah. There have been attempts to explain the missing thousands as members of the northern tribes, women, or children. But the text says nothing about this, and no scholarly explanation has been entirely convincing. For the most part, the opinion among scholars and Bible students is that errors have slipped into the text through copying, due to the special difficulty of understanding and reproducing numerical lists. For a discussion of these problems, see Derek Kidner, *Ezra and Nehemiah: An Introduction and Commentary* (Downers Grove, IL: InterVarsity Press, 1979), 43; and Howard F. Vos, *Bible Study Commentary: Ezra, Nehemiah, and Esther* (Grand Rapids: Zondervan, 1987), 36, 115.

3. Quoted by Barber, in *Nehemiah and the Dynamics of Effective Leadership*, 116.

4. Derek Kidner reflects astutely on what this tells us about how the Law of Moses was being regarded at this time. "The Levites, whom the tithe law treats as greatly outnumbering the priests, had suddenly become a tiny minority with only a fraction of their former claim on the community's support. Yet the law gives them everything, 'every tithe in Israel,' and only requires them to hand on a tenth of this to the priests: 'a tithe of the tithe' (Num. 18:21, 26). Had the law been still in the making or rewriting at this stage, as many have tried to argue, it could never have reached us in this form. To quote Y. Kaufmann, who draws attention to this: 'Nothing proves more clearly how mistaken is the view that in post-exilic times, the Torah book was still being

added to and revised. . . . The founders of post-exilic Judaism were not the composers, but merely the collectors of the Torah literature. They did not alter anything of what they "found written" much less add to it.'" (Kidner, *Ezra and Nehemiah: An Introduction and Commentary*, 40). The Kaufmann quotation is from *The Religion of Israel* (Allen & Unwin, 1961), 193.

Chapter 9

1. Told by Charles Colson with Ellen Santilli Vaughn, in *Kingdoms in Conflict* (Grand Rapids: Zondervan, 1987), 95–108. As Colson indicates, William Wilberforce did go on to abolish other things. After outlawing the slave trade in 1807, Wilberforce fought another eighteen years to emancipate those who were already slaves. He worked for reforms in the prisons and for new laws affecting the poor and the workplace, until ill health eventually forced his retirement from Parliament in 1825.

2. John White, *Excellence in Leadership: Reaching Goals with Prayer, Courage and Determination* (Downers Grove, IL: InterVarsity Press, 1986), 103.

3. Quoted by Cyril J. Barber, in *Nehemiah and the Dynamics of Effective Leadership* (Neptune, NJ: Loizeaux Brothers, 1976), 122.

4. Quoted by William J. Johnson, in *George Washington, the Christian* (Nashville: Abingdon, 1919), 23–28.

5. Quoted by Peter Marshall and David Manuel, in *The Light and the Glory* (Old Tappan, NJ: Revell, 1977), 296.

6. Quoted by Barber, in *Nehemiah and the Dynamics of Effective Leadership*, 112.

7. Ibid.

8. Ibid., 127.

9. The chief support of this view is that running oral translations of the Old Testament later became the normal pattern in synagogue worship. The Targums are the written version of this. Still, we do not know that this was done earlier or even that the people had, for the most part, lost their ability to understand classical Hebrew. Nehemiah's indignation at finding families that could not speak "the language of Judah" when he returned to the city after twelve years (cf. Neh. 13:24) would suggest that in his first term of office Hebrew was generally understood. See Derek Kidner, *Ezra and Nehemiah: An Introduction and Commentary* (Downers Grove, IL: InterVarsity Press, 1979), 106.

10. D. Martyn Lloyd-Jones, *Preaching and Preachers* (Grand Rapids: Zondervan, 1972), 24–25.

Chapter 10

1. Mortimer J. Adler, "Sin," *The Great Ideas: A Syntopicon of Great Books of the Western World*, vol. 2 (Chicago: Encyclopedia Britannica, 1952), 756.

2. John White, *Excellence in Leadership: Reaching Goals with Prayer, Courage and Determination* (Downers Grove, IL: InterVarsity Press, 1986), 114.

3. Derek Kidner, *Ezra and Nehemiah: An Introduction and Commentary* (Downers Grove, IL: InterVarsity Press, 1979), 111.

4. It is an interesting sidelight to this pattern that the prayer moves through the period of the judges up to the time of the monarchy, yet does not mention anything specific about any one of the great Jewish kings, not even King David. Even the recent fall of the two kingdoms to the Assyrians and Babylonians in 721 and 586 BC is at best only vaguely suggested in verse 30. Why are the later events passed over? The answer would seem to be that the later portions of the Old Testament, which chronicle this history, were not yet written or available. Thus they had not been read publicly during these days and were not the basis of the people's meditation and prayers.

5. James Montgomery Boice, *Genesis: An Expositional Commentary*, vol. 1 (Grand Rapids: Baker, 1998), chaps. 5–9.

Chapter 11

1. James B. Pritchard, *Ancient Near Eastern Texts Relating to the Old Testament* (Princeton: Princeton University Press, 1955), 219–23.

2. Howard F. Vos, *Bible Study Commentary: Ezra, Nehemiah, and Esther* (Grand Rapids: Zondervan, 1987), 125.

Chapter 12

1. The city had been destroyed by Nebuchadnezzar in 586 BC and Nehemiah had returned to Jerusalem in 444 BC, building the wall immediately.

2. Ronald J. Sider, "The State of Evangelical Social Concern, 1978," in *Evangelical Newsletter* 5, no. 13 (June 30, 1978).

3. See Howard F. Vos, *Bible Study Commentary: Ezra, Nehemiah, and Esther* (Grand Rapids: Zondervan, 1987), 127.

4. At least some of the those listed as heads of families in verses 12–21 served into the time of Nehemiah, since they are described as from "the days of Joiakim" (v. 12), and the four people mentioned in verse 25 are said to have served both in "the days of Joiakim" and "the days of Nehemiah" (v. 26). So the Uzzi of 11:22 and 12:19 are probably the same person.

5. Cyril J. Barber, *Nehemiah and the Dynamics of Effective Leadership* (Neptune, NJ: Loizeaux Brothers, 1976), 155.

6. Anthony T. Evans, "10 Steps to Urban Renewal," *The Urban Alternative* 4, no. 2 (September 1988).

7. Colonel V. Doner, *The Samaritan Strategy: A New Agenda for Christian Activism* (Brentwood, TN: Wolgemuth & Hyatt, 1988), 37.

8. Raymond J. Bakke, "The Battle for the Cities: What We Have Learned about Urban Evangelization Since Pattaya 1980," *World Evangelization* (March 1986), 16.

Chapter 13

1. J. G. McConville, *Ezra, Nehemiah, and Esther*, in The Daily Study Bible—Old Testament, ed. John C. L. Gibson (Louisville: Westminster/John Knox, 1985), 142.

2. Numbers 8:5–22; 2 Chronicles 35:6; Ezra 6:20; cf. 2 Chronicles 29:15; Nehemiah 13:22; Malachi 3:3.

3. Exodus 19:10; Numbers 19:11–22; Ezekiel 36:25.

4. Exodus 19:14–15.

5. Leviticus 14:48–53.

6. McConville, *Ezra, Nehemiah, and Esther*, 142–43.

Chapter 14

1. Quoted by John R. Noe, in *Peak Performance Principles for High Achievers* (New York: Frederick Fell, 1984), 74.

2. John White, *Excellence in Leadership: Reaching Goals with Prayer, Courage and Determination* (Downers Grove, IL: InterVarsity Press, 1986), 127.

3. Howard F. Vos, *Bible Study Commentary: Ezra, Nehemiah, and Esther* (Grand Rapids: Zondervan, 1987), 134.

4. Cyril J. Barber, *Nehemiah and the Dynamics of Effective Leadership* (Neptune, NJ: Loizeaux Brothers, 1976), 168.

5. White, *Excellence in Leadership*, 123–24.

6. Leighton Ford himself tells this story. I found it in Mariano DiGangi, *Reaching the Unchurched: A Report on the Canadian Consultation on Evangelism* (Scarborough, Canada: Reliable Printing, 1983), 4–5.

Subject Index

Scripture Index

157